Philadelphia Mayor Michael A. Nutter: "Shawn's journey demonstrates a commitment to inspiring others to reach their highest potential while giving back to their communities. I'm proud to see Philadelphians coming together every day in the spirit of volunteerism and Shawn's message reinforces how this spirit can build bridges. Philadelphia is a fitting stop for the Extra Mile America Tour. Among the nation's tenth largest cities, Philadelphia has the highest percentage of workers per capita who commute to work on a bike. We really love bicycling and value its positive impact on personal health and the environment."

Baltimore Mayor Sheila Dixon: "Shawn's journey across this country, finding those in this nation going the extra mile for the benefit of others, is as inspiring in its humanity as it is as a physical feat. As a fellow biker and Mayor of Baltimore, I am pleased Shawn has decided to stop in our city. We are a city full of individuals that go that extra mile every day...for the benefit of our most vulnerable residents and neighbors."

Washington, DC Mayor Adrian M. Fenty: "I commend Shawn on his journey across the country highlighting those individuals who go the extra mile in their communities, and welcome him to the District of Columbia. We share Shawn's vision for giving back to the community through SERVE DC, ...[our] spirit of service through partnerships, national service, and volunteerism."

San Jose City Councilmember Sam Liccardo: "Shawn's solo ride across the country demonstrates that one person going the 'extra mile' can make a difference. The Extra Mile America Tour invites us to bring that spirit to our own community. It's an inspiring commitment to community service."

Greensboro, North Carolina Mayor Yvonne Johnson: "Shawn Anderson serves as an inspiration that reminds us that we are our brother's keeper. I hope we are all inspired to take up our own individual journey to refocus our lives on what is truly important."

Seattle Council President Richard Conlin: "Seattle is a city of people who exemplify the volunteer spirit. And Shawn Anderson is someone who...demonstrate[s] that community service is indeed the life blood of a community. He shines a light on what truly matters in our community; that nonprofit organizations provide invaluable service to those in need."

San Francisco Mayor Gavin Newsom: "As host to the National Conference on Volunteering and Service, San Francisco embodies the spirit of making a difference. Our city is the perfect starting line for Shawn Anderson's Extra Mile America Tour. One person riding his bike across the country—helping to shine the light on local heroes and organizations such as Project Homeless Connect —inspires us all to go the extra mile, help someone, and acknowledge those tirelessly working in the trenches."

Dublin, Ohio Mayor Marilee Chinnici-Zuercher: "Shawn Anderson inspires us and reminds us what it means to go the 'extra mile' in our everyday lives. I encourage everyone to go the distance by volunteering to lend a hand."

Pittsburgh Mayor Luke Ravenstahl: "Pittsburghers know how important it is to give back, as was illustrated...when well over 1,000 citizens came out to assist with litter pick-ups and other activities to green our City. Shawn's de[illegible] literally, as he bikes across the country is a reminder...I [illegible] to follow Shawn's lead, go the extra mile, and donate th[illegible]

Columbus Mayor Michael B. Coleman: "Columbus is known for our tradition of assisting the most vulnerable members of our community, and we are honored to be part of Shawn Anderson's inspirational...journey. I urge all citizens to join Shawn in going the extra mile and giving back through community involvement and volunteerism."

Fayetteville, Arkansas Mayor Lioneld Jordan: "As Mayor of Fayetteville, I am grateful to Shawn Anderson for biking many miles on a path of inspiration that is capturing America. Shawn's tribute to volunteerism and the many volunteers who have made our communities, states, and nation great is commendable and inspirational. When we go the extra mile, we increase value in our own lives, our communities, our environment, and in the quality of life for others. Way to go!"

Honolulu Councilmember Ikaika Anderson: "Aloha is a special word that means both 'hello' and 'goodbye.' Aloha means, 'We love you.'...'I'll be there for you.' It has never been more important than right now that we all exemplify the true meaning of Aloha. Shawn Anderson is doing just that in his goal to reach out across America in public service to his comrades and his country. Shawn's Extra Mile Tour...is his invitation to everyone who is able to pitch in to help our neighbors, to share what is ours, to boost our economy, and to be better citizens. Honolulu extends its Aloha to Shawn...."

Nampa, Idaho Mayor Tom Dale: "Shawn...shows us that nothing can stop us from going the extra mile in our own lives. Shawn Anderson's...Tour reminds us of the importance of acknowledging our local heroes and following in their footsteps. The residents of Nampa, Idaho embody this 'extra mile' spirit."

Salt Lake City Mayor Ralph Becker: "Going the extra mile is what our City is all about. With a rich history and tradition of volunteerism...our community appreciates the sacrifices and the benefits of serving our neighbors. Shawn's visit will strike a chord with...local everyday heroes and will no doubt inspire more of us to go that extra mile."

Oakland Mayor Ron Dellums: "The challenges of our current times have demonstrated to all Americans that now, more than ever, it is necessary for us to work in cooperation to achieve real change in our communities. Shawn Anderson's unique undertaking is an inspiration to all Americans to reach beyond the ordinary and truly achieve their own 'extra mile.' As a pioneering force in creating a new green energy economy, Oakland's vision as a model city embodies the goals of the Extra Mile America Tour, reflecting our belief that the motivation and hard work of our citizens is the key to building a better future."

Congresswoman Doris Matsui, U.S. House of Representatives: "In these times of need, many Sacramentans are going the extra mile to make a genuine difference in our community. We are thrilled Shawn Anderson is including our city on his Extra Mile America Tour, and I know that he will find many local heroes throughout Sacramento. Volunteerism and service strengthen our communities, foster respect and compassion throughout our society, and make a real difference in the lives of both those who serve and those who benefit from their service."

Congresswoman Lynn Woolsey, U.S. House of Representatives: "People like Shawn Anderson show us that when we push beyond what we think our limitations may be—we can inspire others to do the same. As our nation faces extraordinary challenges together, Shawn's solo ride across the country, and the Extra Mile America Tour, invites every American to find the 'Extra Mile" inside, and bring that spirit forth in his or her own community—proving that one person really can make a difference."

Extra Mile America:

Stories of Inspiration, Possibility and Purpose

SHAWN ANDERSON

Foreword by Kevin Johnson, Sacramento Mayor and Former NBA All-Star

Also by Shawn Anderson:
Countdown to College: Preparing Your Student for Success in the Collegiate Universe
SOAR to the TOP: Rise Above the Crowd and Fly Away to Your Dream
Amicus 101: A Story About the Pursuit of Purpose and Overcoming Life's Chaos
Lessons From A. Friend: A Guided Journal Through the Lessons of Amicus 101

Extra Mile America: Stories of Inspiration, Possibility and Purpose
by Shawn Anderson

ISBN: 978-0-9820974-2-7

Printed in the United States of America
Limited First Printing

cover artist: Rosella Lucherino; *photographer:* Julian Walter;

book design: Dawn King - set in Adobe Garamond Pro, Bradley Hand, Arial

Published by

Goldmind Press®™

Goldmind Press
Marina del Rey, CA 90292
USA

Order this book online at www.ShawnAnderson.com

Library of Congress Control Number: 2010920957

To Christine...

No one makes
"going the extra mile"
look more natural.

EXTRA MILE AMERICA TOUR
THE 21 CITIES

1. *San Francisco, CA (July 21)*
2. *Oakland, CA (July 22)*
3. *Sacramento, CA (July 24)*
4. *Reno, NV (July 27)*
5. *Salt Lake City, UT (Aug. 5)*
6. *Denver, CO (Aug. 17)*
7. *Omaha, NE (Aug. 27)*
8. *Des Moines, IA (Aug. 31)*
9. *Chicago, IL (Sept. 8)*
10. *Ft. Wayne, IN (Sept. 11)*
11. *Columbus , OH (Sept. 16)*
12. *Pittsburgh, PA (Sept. 22)*
13. *Washington, DC (Oct. 1)*
14. *Baltimore, MD (Oct. 5)*
15. *Wilmington, DE (Oct. 7)*
16. *Philadelphia, PA (Oct. 9)*
17. *Newark, NJ (Oct. 12)*
18. *New York City, NY (Oct. 14)*
19. *Hartford, CT (Oct. 16)*
20. *Providence, RI (Oct. 19)*
21. *Boston, MA (Oct. 23)*

CONTENTS

My deepest heartfelt thanks
to all the extra mile people who helped create this book and the Extra Mile America Tour [in no particular order]:

Christine Anderson, Annika Ihnat, Dawn King, Debra Amador, Julian Walter, Jinx Kennedy, Rhoda Orbe, Laura Trout, Daisy Larrios, Giovanna Brandi, Sean Young, Gabriel Koneta, Rosella Lucherino.

Sponsors: Joie De Vivre Hotels, Best Western, Enterprise Rent-A-Car, GreekBox.com, Brandings.com, Clif Bar, Jelly Belly, Adventure Cycling Assoc.

Mayor Kevin Johnson and Joaquin McPeek - Media & Communications Coordinator, Office of Mayor Kevin Johnson (Sacramento, CA); Carla Markell, First Lady of Delaware; HandsOn Network; Gail Myers, Sr. Advisor to Councilmember Ikaika Anderson (Honolulu, HI); Kathy Dixon, Aide to Councilmember Rodney Glassman (Tucson, AZ); Peggy Shaver, Assistant to Mayor Tom Dale (Nampa, ID); Linda Trout, Community Services Manager, Omaha Public Library (Omaha, NE); Teri Munger, Volunteer Sacramento (CA); Jean Joley, Executive Director, Volunteer Center @ RSVP (Fort Wayne, IN); Marilee Chinnici-Zuercher, President/CEO, FIRSTLINK (Columbus, OH); Eric Brandon, Policy Advisor to Mayor Michael B. Coleman (Columbus, OH); Alexa New, Program Manager of Campus Cares (Pittsburgh, PA); Clare Garrison, Volunteer Services Coordinator, State Office of Volunteerism (Wilmington, DE); Ellen Firestone, Sr. Finance & Communications Executive, Greater Philadelphia Cares (PA).

Sherry Lynn Fazio, Sr. Director of External Affairs, Jersey Cares (Newark, NJ); Rosemary Aiello, Director of Fund Development, HandsOn Hartford (CT); Janice Pothier Pac, Director of Volunteer Center & Community Services, Serve Rhode Island (Providence, RI); Juli Green, Nevada Casting (Reno, NV); Marla Kennedy, Deputy Communications Director, Mayor Ralph Becker's Office (Salt Lake City, UT); Kristy Judd, Executive Director, Metro Volunteers (Denver, CO); Shirley Burgess, Director of Volunteer Engagement, United Way of Central Iowa (Des Moines, IA); Rory Hackbarth, Chicago Cares (IL).

Michael Limmer, VP of Marketing, Ft. Wayne TinCaps (IN); Melissa Rapp, Marketing & Media Relations Consultant, FIRSTLINK (Columbus, OH); Sarah Fleischer, Director of Communications and Special Events, Greater DC Cares (Washington, DC); Kelly Hodge-Williams, Executive Director, Business Volunteers Unlimited Maryland (Baltimore, MD); Marsha Reeves-Jews, Director of Events, Frederick Douglass Isaac Myers Maritime Park (Baltimore, MD).

Colleen Farrell, Senior Director of Marketing and Communications, New York Cares (NY); Kelley Rice, VP of External Affairs, YMCA Greater Boston (MA), and the two hundred extra mile Americans who inspired me with their stories.

FOREWORD

BY KEVIN JOHNSON,
MAYOR OF SACRAMENTO & FORMER NBA ALL-STAR

Two life-changing principles were hammered home during my formative years growing up in Sacramento. First was the idea of working hard and going the extra mile in everything I pursued. I knew that if I wanted to achieve a goal, I needed to do more than the average person. I needed to push hard, study hard, and never forget the importance of repetitive practice.

Second was the principle that I should give back to both my community and my country. Growing up, my grandfather told me a good person can't sit on the sideline. He taught me that my greatest reward and contribution as an individual would be measured by my service and how others could benefit from my actions.

Both concepts became an integral part of everything I did and pursued. In following these principles, I've had the great fortune of achieving a number of goals important to me: I graduated from the University of California at Berkeley; played in the National Basketball Association for 13 years; founded a non-profit community-development organization focused on turning my hometown's inner-city communities into centers of hope and possibility; and I was elected the Mayor of Sacramento. I am proud of each one of these goals.

I take Shawn Anderson's *go the extra mile* message to heart, and I am pleased to write the Foreword for his book, *Extra Mile America: Stories of Inspiration, Possibility and Purpose*. His message reflects the same themes that make Sacramento great.

One of my first acts after being elected Mayor was to launch a volunteer initiative encouraging citizens to give back to our city. The citizens of California's State Capitol stepped up and responded with deep conviction. In the first year of the initiative, our city generated three times more volunteer hours than we had set as our initial goal.

However, this was a goal where success was measured not only by total hours volunteered, but demonstrated by the powerful and positive effects that come from people rallying around a cause greater than themselves. We came together as one to achieve the goal of making Sacramento the most caring city in California.

When Shawn pedaled to Sacramento during his *Extra Mile America Tour*, he met some of our city's inspiring residents and recognized them for their extraordinary contributions. I was happy to have the opportunity to meet Shawn during the event. His unique way of highlighting a special message and desire to serve and encourage others made his tour something I was proud to support.

I personally commend Shawn for his willingness to get off the bench and into the game. At a time when resources are scarce but needs are great, we need people like Shawn to inspire us all on to do more. And that's what he is doing.

He is encouraging all of us to stand up and ask, "How can I help?" My hope is that people will read this book and be inspired to answer the call to serve—as a family member, as a friend, as a professional, and as a member of their community. We live in a great country and it only gets better when we go the extra mile.

Join the mission. Do your part. Serve.

TWO DATES...ONE PEN

It's Never Crowded On The Extra Mile
...Roger Staubach

Tom Tuohy, the founder of ***Dreams for Kids*** shared the quote with me in Chicago. He was one of six people in the city I interviewed, and one of over two hundred *extra mile heroes* I spoke with as I pedaled a bike solo over four thousand miles across the country.

The Staubach quote summarizes so much of the *Extra Mile America* story. It speaks of the unique courage and the bold confidence that so many of the people I met on the tour shared. It speaks of my own passion to give life my all.

Far more than a challenging bike ride, the ***Extra Mile America Tour*** was created as a reminder that life's greatest challenges are overcome...and its sweetest successes experienced...when we *go the extra mile* in life. This book tells not only the story of my own *extra mile adventure*, but more importantly, it highlights the stories of twenty-five amazing heroes I met and interviewed along the route. It is their stories that kept my tired legs moving then...and it is their stories that inspire me now..

Often life can be challenging and we feel like getting off our own metaphorical bike. Tired legs, flat tires, strong headwinds, a pouring rain, steep hills...that's life at times, isn't it?

Perhaps you are at a place in life where your own legs are tired from seeming to be always pedaling up hill in your own version of the Rockies. If so, the stories in this book are sure to inspire you to re-evaluate your situation, take one more deep breath of courage, get back on your own life bike and keep pedaling with a renewed passion and purpose.

In life, we are each given two dates…neither of which we have much say in determining. Those two dates mark our short existence on earth and represent our beginning…and our ending. If we are lucky, however, in between those dates will be thousands of other dates, too. It is those dates that are the most important. It is on those dates where our individual life stories are written.

As you read these pages, it is my hope that either my adventure or the collection of stories from people whom I met will inspire you to look at your own life story a bit more closely and remember that there are still more amazing dates to be lived…and purposeful chapters to be written. It's also to remind you that **you** control the pen.

Getting through life is a lot like riding a bike across the country. Every day there are new hills to climb and long distances to be covered. Every day we have the choice to either *ride* or *not ride*. But success on a cross-country bike ride…and in life…requires finding the motivation to get off the curb when we are tired and to find the will to get back on those two wheels. It requires getting up every day…despite the weather…despite the aches…despite the previous day's crash…despite flat tires…despite everything.

And if we are to do either successfully…ride a bike across the country or live a great life…we will be required to *go the extra mile.*

IT DOESN'T HAVE TO BE THIS WAY!

I wanted to do something big.

It seemed like the times required it. Dark news seemed to be everywhere, and people were depressed by what was going on around them. Unemployment rates were over ten percent and climbing. People I knew were losing their homes and having a tough time paying bills. Friends were struggling in relationships. Lifetime savings accounts had been pummeled by Wall Street's greed. Businesses all around...even banks...were closing. A shroud of negativity seemed to be cloaking positive thought, and optimism seemed to be falling into a dark abyss.

It was easy to get caught up in the noise. It was easy to feel down. It was easy to feel as if the world was out of control and there was nothing that we could do. The un-empowering twin brothers of "helplessness" and "hopelessness" seemed to be smirking through the life window of so many...arrogantly mouthing the words:

"*We got you!*"

Besides the reversal of tone that had replaced America's naturally optimistic spirit, a second transition was also taking place in the country. A new president had entered the White House.

To me, it really didn't matter what political party had lined up behind him, the new guy seemed to have his finger on what I felt was a critically important element in re-directing America's confidence recovery:

Restore hope.

To me, that was a national positive. My personal belief system shouted out internally that if individual hope was restored, the hope of the country would collectively follow.

As I listened closely to the new President's words, I heard a personal challenge:

What are you doing to make a difference?

The message challenged me hard, and I came to the conclusion that I wasn't doing enough; I wanted to do more. I wanted to join the army of hope givers and make a difference for others... but how?

My small, encouraging "***It doesn't have to be this way!***" voice might not do a whole bunch on the big scale, but I did believe that I could affect a lot of people one-by-one and in that way contribute to getting positive momentum flowing again.

I set my sights on using my single voice to whisper passionately to as many people as I could.

EMPOWERING 1,000,000 PEOPLE

As I melted my thought and value process down in order to give shape to what this "big thing" might be, I kept coming back again and again to my overall life mission:

> ***Empower a million people to lead a more positive and purposeful existence.***

The power of an encouraging "*Nice job!*" can be life-changing. It can be all that is needed to inspire someone else to boldly walk the path to their true life purpose. An encouraging word can give someone the courage to fulfill a dream or maximize the potential of a moment. Receiving an empowering slap on the back causes us to push a bit harder, to dig a bit deeper, to run a bit faster…and in the end…to share our value with the world a bit more.

Unfortunately, we live in a world where encouragement is shared too little. "*You can't!*" is a much more commonly shared sentiment than "*You can!*" Negative feedback has never been a very good source of promoting extra strength, will, or effort.

When we take the constant drilling of "*No!*" to heart, it is easy to lose faith and confidence in our abilities. It is easy to lose sight of motivating goals and life dreams. Sometimes we begin to actually believe that going for a goal is not worth the risk or that we couldn't do it even if we tried.

I believe that planted deeply within every single person is the seed of something extraordinary. It has nothing to do with fame, power, or money…and everything to do with contribution and adding value to others. Because of this, I set my vision on being the "*Go for it!*" guy. I make it my purpose to be the encourager that says:

> ***"Yes, you can!"***

Following a life mission statement has given me a renewed sense of what to do in moments when I hesitate and wonder, *What's next?* In the case of planning the *Extra Mile America Tour,* my life mission became the heartbeat of everything that I would eventually decide and do. It became the purpose that built the steps and the passion that pushed me up them.

If you don't have a life mission, I highly recommend creating one. If you do have one, **don't be afraid to share it with others.**

After all, it could be life-changing for both parties.

THE *GO THE EXTRA MILE* MESSAGE

Despite the negative, ongoing financial crisis that was caving in the spirit of so many, I felt that there was something positive that I could do—and that each of us could do—to change the mood of the currently depressing tune. I believed there was a message that needed to be shared and had the power to rejuvenate the human spirit, one that could turn "helplessness" into determined action and "hopelessness" into confidence that tomorrow would be better.

The four-word message was powerfully simple:

"Go the extra mile!"

The quality of our lives depends on the effort we put into our lives; it is our thoughts, our attitudes, and our actions that are the real determiners of our lives' directions. The course our individual lives take is of our own choosing. It isn't the banks, the government, our boss, or our friends who are in control of our destiny.

It is us!

Being a big dreamer in heart and mind, I have experienced my fair share of ugly losses, negative rejections and confidence-cracking disappointments. I know what it is to struggle, what it is to fail, what it is to feel pain; I know what it is to pray:

"*Oh God…now what am I going to do?*"

It has been my experience that in times of failure, loss, pain and struggle…isolation can be a very seductive enemy that has the power to sink his teeth into our very confidence and will. BUT I also have experienced the opposite. I know what it takes to dust myself off…dream one more time…and go for it again. I know what it is to restore hope in myself. I know what it takes to get up one more time…and this time…win.

Getting off the canvas after a knockdown requires shaking off the memory of the fall. It requires a little extra arm push to get back to your knees, and then steadying shaky legs in order to rise back to your feet. The boxing metaphor is a perfect description for *how to succeed in life.*

When our goals are big, there is an excellent chance we will be met by initial failure. Eventual success requires an extra push in time and effort. For very few, success is automatic. For most of us, success requires us to engage 100% in utilizing in unison our brains, our time, and our guts.

For me, this has definitely proven true. My biggest paychecks, my best accomplishments, my best everything has always come when I have dug a bit deeper in my bag of resources. For all of us, it doesn't matter if our discouragement is related to our finances, careers, health, or our relationships…the answer to getting back on track is the same:

Don't quit. Try harder. Dig deeper.

Never has success or positive results been obtained by lying low…doing less…or even quitting. Always is it found in doing more. Always is it found in *going the extra mile.*

PUTTING IT ALL TOGETHER

Empowering people...going the extra mile...making a difference...stepping out of my comfort zone...eventually, all my ideas and goals came together. The final plan might have seemed unrealistic to some, but to me, it seemed like an amazing challenge.

Here's the final 3 BIG details of the *Extra Mile America Tour:*

1. The Ride:

I would pedal a bicycle...solo...from San Francisco to Boston. Sure, pedaling across the United States was a long way and an intense goal...but I needed a symbol...something that showed what "*go the extra mile*" really meant. Over ninety days pedaling ocean-to-ocean illustrated that objective very clearly.

NOTE:
As far as the actual "making it across" part, I was never seriously worried if I could make it. Even though I was only a recreational runner and not a cyclist, I had confidence in my ability to complete the journey. I knew my legs were strong...and my will was even stronger. The challenging part for me, however, was psychological. Looking at a United States map in its entirety caused me problems. My brain would then routinely start to freak out and shout, "Are you kidding?" I would stick to looking at only state maps.

2. The People:

I would zig-zag my way up, down and across the country visiting twenty-one major cities. In those cities, I would interview *extra mile Americans* who were kindred spirits in their *extra mile* belief system. Despite setbacks in their own personal lives, these people had gotten back up and had done something great. For some, it was overcoming unbelievable tragedies. For others, it was following through with a deep-seeded dream. In both cases, I desired to recognize their *extra-mile stories.*

NOTE:
The final route I chose had no significant meaning, but was more of an effort to include as many states and big cities as possible. The starting spot, San Francisco, was close to home and that felt comfortable. On the other side of the country, Boston was about as high up the East Coast as I could imagine. In hitting a spot in the northern part of the country, Chicago became my choice. It seemed reasonable to think that if this trip was all about going the extra mile, dreaming big, and creating possibility, what better place to include than the hometown of Oprah?

3. The Day:

I would develop political and community leader support for establishing November 1st as "***Extra Mile Day***" in cities across the country. This would be a day that service to others, volunteerism, and having an *extra mile spirit* would be highlighted. Establishing a special commemorative day was an opportunity to enlist the help of others in spreading the *extra mile* message in cities I would not be able to visit.

NOTE:
I knew I wanted to establish "Extra Mile Day" on a date after the Tour was completed. Ending in late October, there were limited choices. In the end, I just liked the idea of three ones lined up together...11/1. There was something that seemed lucky about it to me.

Journal Entry January 18:
What am I going to do? How can I make a difference? If I am going to do something...I want to be unique and use my full voice. I can't be afraid, and I don't want a watered-down idea. Why be ordinary when I know I am capable of doing the extra-ordinary? Keep thinking, keep pushing...and make this B-I-G!

BLESSINGS

Sometimes, it's easy to ignore how rich our individual lives are.

We seem to get so caught up in looking at everything we don't have, that we forget all the blessings we do have. It's easy to forget how awesome it is to have sight...when we aren't blind. It's easy to forget how great it is to walk...when we aren't in a wheelchair. It's easy to forget how lucky we are to have a bed at night...when we aren't sleeping on the streets.

I suppose we have become a non-appreciative culture...always wanting more...not appreciating what we do have. I know I have often stood in the front of that line.

But it's a shame.

I was in San Francisco on Day One of the Tour. I thought it would be a good idea to start my cross-country trip with my heart in the right place...with an attitude of appreciation and gratitude and less worry about the outcome of everything...so I volunteered early in the morning to serve breakfast at ***Glide Memorial.*** *Glide* is one of the country's largest food and homeless shelters, and in 2009, they served an outrageous number of meals...950,000 to be exact. For those reaching for a calculator to do the math breakdown (I did), that's an average of 2,600 meals a day. Having assisted in serving one simple meal on the front-line, let me share that there is nothing simple about serving over 800 breakfasts. It takes a true *extra mile effort.*

To add a layer of background for *Glide Memorial,* movie buffs may remember the homeless shelter as being the inspirational venue behind the Will Smith movie *Pursuit of Happyness.* Will plays a real life, rags-to-riches, homeless-to-millionaire gentleman named Chris Gardner. The true story is that Chris and his young son struggled mightily up the economic ladder and were forced to live at *Glide* for a short time. Without this organization's assistance, Chris's stirring story might not have ever been written.

I thought *Glide* was a perfect place to start my crossing-the-country story, too.

There was little doubt that I was humbled greatly by what I experienced by serving that morning. When I left my two-hour shift, my heart was fully reminded of the life blessings I had been given, but so readily forget. I had been serving homeless families…with little children…who had nowhere else to go for a meal, and just prior to helping, I was stressing about whether or not my cross-country, *extra-mile experiment* was going to make a dent in the world.

Sometimes…when we pay attention…the Universe reminds us of our blessings. Today, I was paying attention.

When I left *Glide*, I decided to walk the one and a quarter miles back to my hotel where I would be jumping into my first interviews in a few hours. While walking, I recalled the smiling face of a thankful little four-year-old from earlier that morning. She had been at *Glide* with just her mom, and both were so grateful every time I would bring coffee or milk. Each time I stopped by their table, the little precious heart pulled her milk cup away from her mouth and whispered, "*Thank you.*" If you have ever had a moment in your life where your heart yanks its way up from your chest cavity to your throat and then simultaneously triggers your tear ducts… well…that was one of those moments for me.

And it kept happening all morning.

As I walked back, I was thinking of that little girl with her cute milk mustache. She was so grateful and her smile was so sweet. It was easy for me to imagine the possibility that maybe…just maybe…she could even be a real-life angel sent down to help guide all of us big people to get our acts together. At the very least…on this day…for at least one big person in the world...she was a real-life earth angel. As I walked back in the cool morning air, I was still wet with sweat from having run back and forth at *Glide* serving as many as I could. And although the wet perspiration and the cool air started to chill my outsides, my heart was tender warm because of my morning experience.

But little girl number one is only part of the story. There was a second little girl. I would see little girl number two as I was heading back to the hotel on my walk.

Heading up one of the long, hilly San Francisco streets, I passed a Montessori school. A mother was dropping off her daughter… roughly the same age as the tiny angel I had met…at school for the day while she, it appeared, headed off to work. This little girl was crying and didn't seem excessively appreciative of her surroundings or what was happening in her little world. There was nothing horrible about the moment. It was the sharpness of this contrast to the previous encounter that had significance.

The contrast between the two girls struck me hard. One had been born into a life of what seemed to be financial privilege. The other was born into a world of economic survival. It's tough not to wonder why one little girl was born into a world of so much…and the other wasn't.

It didn't seem fair. But often, that's just how life is.

Isn't it?

We can spend all the time in the world complaining about what we don't have and what we deserve. We can look at those who were born into wealth or who had an enormously lucky life break and think, *Why wasn't that me?* We can wish all we want, but the bottom line is we are each a hundred times more lucky than millions of others on this planet.

I have food in my refrigerator, clothes in my closet, and a bed tonight. Do you? Roughly 75% of the world's population struggles with this.

The fact that you are reading this speaks loudly…first to the fact that you can read, and second to the fact that you are still alive. Two billion people can't read, and one million people won't make it through the week.

Gulp!

Do you have a $5 bill in your wallet or somewhere at home? If so, congratulations. You are one of the richest 8% of the people in the world.

Those are called blessings, my friend. Take away any one of them from your world and watch how fast you wish your life was just as it is today.

We are far more fortunate than we ever realize.

But maybe it's time we start realizing it. More.

Maybe it's time we take a note from the little angel's life playbook and whisper back into the Universe:

"*Thank you.*"

P.S. Nearing the hotel and the interviews, my thoughts were abruptly shaken back to the here-and-now. As I waited at a stop walk for the crossing light to change, three young teenagers were standing with me waiting to cross the street. One of them turned and asked me a question, "Wanna' buy some pot?"

Sometimes in life we are blessed...yes. And other times in life, our choices determine our blessings.

EXTRA MILE HERO

You're Not Invisible

...the photographer who sees everybody

Joe Ramos is an amazing photographer.

When you see a face that has been captured by his magic camera, you immediately believe that Joe Ramos is living his purpose. Flipping through Joe's portfolio of portraits, I felt the same building emotion as I would flipping through the pages of *Time Magazine's Year in Review*. Joe's portraits just flat out move you.

Looking at the faces of his camera's targets, you feel things. You feel the lives of the people whom his lens has captured. In their eyes...in their faces...Joe's work tells a life story without words. His photographs see beyond the smile; they see into the life of the person. The good times...the bad times...you feel them. A Joe Ramos photograph just doesn't capture beauty and ego, it captures life.

At an early age, Joe developed a lasting sensitivity towards those who were struggling and doing their best to find a foot-hold niche in life. Born to Mexican and Filipino labor camp working parents, Joe grew up living and working in the California agriculture fields in the Salinas Valley. Wages were low; there was no health insurance, and many of the simple standards we all take for granted in our homes today were absent in those communal living environments. When winters came and work was scarce, Joe's father often had to borrow money from the single men in the labor camp who didn't have a family to support. Survival was the focus.

Remembering those early days of struggle...remembering how hard life can be...how important it is to step forward and help someone else...those lessons still live with Joe Ramos, now age sixty. The deep-seeded compassion for how hard some people have to work to survive has never left him. He doesn't forget his roots.

Nobody should ever feel invisible.

Six times a year, Joe Ramos makes a visit to San Francisco's ***Project Homeless Connect.*** During those visits, Joe takes his God-given talent and the lessons he learned growing up…and he gives back to those who are struggling. He takes photographic portraits of the homeless and makes them feel visible once again. In fact, he has taken over a thousand portraits.

What makes it special about shooting a homeless person's picture? Lots.

Nobody should ever feel invisible in life, and Joe Ramos does what he can to make sure that the homeless of San Francisco can be seen. With his time, his talent, and his money, Joe Ramos gives back visibility. At his expense, he clicks, develops and hands back what he shoots. He mails the portraits to general delivery addresses. He mails them to family members so that they will know "their" person is still visible.

In life, sometimes it is so easy to disappear in a crowd. Sometimes it is easy to feel as if you are just a number in a society of other numbers. Call a service vendor and the first thing you are asked for is your account number. We are becoming a world of numbers…and in doing so…a bit of our humanity seems to be escaping. Imagine how much more that feeling must be magnified when you are alone in this world and on the streets.

Joe Ramos' roots remind him of the importance of being seen. That's why he sets out to acknowledge others in the most decent and human way he can.

I see you, my friend. You matter. Let me take your picture.

EXTRA MILE HERO

For Those Who Think, "I Can't"

...a modern day superman

I met him in Oakland, California.

Little did I know at the time, but the inspiration behind that thirty-minute meeting would subsequently carry me over the Sierra Nevada Mountains and across the Nevada desert in heat over 110 degrees.

"*If Creighton can...I can!*"

The self-spoken words greeted my every giant pedal push on the bike as I passed one elevation marker after another all the way to the top of the Sierra's over 8,900 foot Carson Pass.

So who is this inspiration? Who exactly is Creighton Wong?

For starters, Creighton Wong is an extraordinarily self-empowered human being. He thinks and talks and lives with an attitude a bit different from the rest of us. He just believes he can do whatever he sets his mind upon doing.

All the time.

What makes Creighton so extraordinarily special is that he walks...let me correct that...*he swims and bikes and runs* through life with an attitude that is as powerfully positive as any human being I have ever met. I suppose when you're a tri-athlete, exercising one to two hours a day, four days a week, you have to carry that sort of motivation with you. Any of us who have struggled to get on the treadmill for twenty minutes for just one day a week can relate to the sort of positive energy it takes just to get off the couch.

Some days, it takes a massive amount.

But Creighton does more than the casual twenty minute treadmill spin. He swims a mile. He rides a bike for 25 miles. He then runs for another 6 miles. The swim...the bike ride...the run...

he does them all together one after the other. Heck, I love exercise and the benefits that come with it, but I think his regimen is an awesome test of physical fitness.

Oh...and by the way...Creighton Wong is a congenital amputee.

Being born without a right leg, and missing three fingers on his left hand and two fingers on his right hand, is no big deal to Creighton. He doesn't over analyze the situation and think, *I can't do that.* He just finds a way. He never feels sorry for himself and wishes things were different. He just doesn't. He accepts and moves forward.

"*The 'I wish' game is a dangerous game. I am much more appreciative of things just watching how they unfold.*"

Born in 1973, Creighton has always played sports...soccer, little league baseball, basketball, volleyball, four square...everything. Today, he races for the ***Challenged Athletes Foundation*** and fundraises for young children who are amputees so that they may have access to prosthetics, and thus, the ability to compete in whatever sport they choose.

Creighton has taken his "difference"...what many of us would have considered a reason to throw in the towel...and has turned it into something positive. In doing so, he has naturally elevated himself into a real life super hero...for young amputees, for wounded soldiers, for cancer survivors, for accident victims...for all of us with two legs.

"*Sure there were times when the bad days outnumbered the good; when the failures outnumbered the successes. But in every failure is an opportunity to learn and I've learned two things: How to fall...and how to pick myself up. Honestly, I'm not smart enough to know how to quit. I really just don't know how to do it.*"

Thank you, Creighton.

Thank you for not knowing how to quit. Thank you for pushing past pre-conceived limitations. Thank you for helping me to climb every mountain pass and make it across the country on a bike. Thank you for being a true *extra mile American.*

And thank you, too, for your words:

"***I can!***"

WHY?

Why?

That question and its multiple variations is one I have heard a hundred times.

"*Are you crazy? Why would you want to ride your bike across the country?*"

Regardless of the day and length of time I was given to explain myself, the answer has always been more complicated than the question.

Why? Because I wanted to show others that despite a world of negative news, there are still great things going on.

Why? Because even though it is easy to feel powerless in a world where events seem to be dictated to us, there is still the possibility that opportunity is just waiting for us to create.

Why? Because I wanted to push myself to another level of performance and result. I wanted to grow as a person.

Why? Because I wanted to make a difference and contribute.

Why? Because I wanted to cast a light on people who were doing great things.

I had tens of "*Why?*" answers.

Deep down, though, my answer to myself was as simple as it gets: ***I have but one life.***

At the end…when I am sitting in my rocking chair reflecting back upon my own life story, I want to feel good about what I am remembering.

EXTRA MILE HERO

82% Of Your Profits?
...the man dedicated to: *Give Something Back*

Mike Hannigan is a business owner cut out of the rarest cloth. And I mean the very rarest. Why? Because he gives most of his company's profits away.

Now who in the world does that?

To be exact, Mike has given back 82% of his company's profit. If 82% doesn't strike your "*Wow!*" button...how about this fact: over the course of his business' eighteen year history, he has given a whopping $4.5 million in donations to the community.

He didn't have to give any of it away. But he did.

In my world, that is true *extra mile generosity*. In Mike's world, it's the way it is supposed to be. Sure, Mike would have been a hero in many books by meeting that magical ten percent number we have grown up hearing...but not to himself. Too small. Not enough. Mike believes we are called to do more. To him, it's not a religious thing; it's a human being thing.

One day...years ago...Mike was in a grocery store and picked up a bottle of salad dressing distributed by a famous fellow named Paul Newman. The late actor was big on pushing the "give back" concept with his own line of food products, and when Mike heard that, it struck a mental and emotional chord. "*I can do that!*" Being a man of great action and conviction, Mike started doing exactly that.

Mike started a business selling office products called:

Give Something Back.

And ever since…he has been giving…a lot of…"something back."

Shawn: "*So, Mike, why not just spend the money on yourself and enjoy life a bit more?*"

Mike: "*If money was the most important thing in life, I would. But it isn't. What is far more important is finding a way to use the power of my business to create social benefits and support community interests.*"

Heady thinking, huh? But frankly, that's what matters most… that's the bottom line for Mike Hannigan…***helping the community.***

Mike runs his customer-centered business, maximizes profits, and then spreads the money out to organizations that need cash to survive. In 2008, 110 different organizations benefitted. Over the course of *Give Something Back* history…over 4,000 organizations have been given an additional financial breath.

Another truly unique piece in all of this is that Mike doesn't even really think of the profit the business makes as his to begin with. In his bold eyes, not only does the "community" have a seat at Mike's shareholders' table, he believes the community is the central shareholder.

"*The profits of every company go somewhere,*" Mike shares. "*I am just redistributing mine. Everybody agrees there are important societal problems to be solved. I've just found a way to work on some of them by mastering the ability to connect financial resources with community need.*"

So what's next for *Give Something Back*?

Well, Mike has added an immediate challenge to his life mission of helping others. He has a goal of providing 25,000 backpacks loaded with essential school supplies to kids floating under the poverty line in two Bay Area counties…Contra Costa and Alameda.

"*It's a start,*" says Mike. "*After all, there are a 170,000 kids under the line who need school supplies. And who knows…but maybe next year, we can reach 40,000 kids.*"

It's hard for me to even register that such selflessness can actually be real in today's world. But Mike Hannigan's is real. His generosity and community concern is not a one-time thing, either…it's his adopted way of life.

I was lucky to meet Mike, and no doubt his "community first" lesson has been planted into my brain. It's a good way to live. Maybe, just maybe, I can…we all can…find a way to try to follow Mike's example.

Is there any doubt that the world would be a better place if we did?

P.S. It should be noted that in the first 18 years of its existence, this green-oriented, price-leading, office supply selling company is the largest independently owned business in its field in the western states. Do you think, maybe, Mike is onto a business success secret here?

BELIEVE...PART 1

Sometimes...no matter what others may say...you have to find that place inside yourself that truly believes in "I can."

The following is a July 6th e-mail sent to me fifteen days before I started "*Day One*" of the ride:

"*Listen, Shawn, I don't want to deflate your bicycle tires, but I've got to say that I am very concerned about the viability of the Tour at this stage. The fact that you don't have the sponsors you'd hoped for -- and got so many NOs in a row -- well, I think it's something to look at.*

Sometimes the Universe gives you signs so that you can alter your course and take another road. This could mean postponing the tour and doing it when you have the support you really need/want. I know timing is a big piece of this, but I am seriously concerned about your well-being and ability to do this with so little support. I have no idea how much money you have spent thus far. And I know this is not your main motivator or concern. So, I am asking you to consider what I am saying before that release goes out. No one would fault you for postponing and regrouping at this stage. And I would of course help you do it gracefully, leaving the possibilities open for another road. I am not abandoning you, Shawn. But my gut told me to address this with you before it's too late. Please consider what I've said and let's talk in the morning."

BELIEVE...PART 2

It was July 18th, three days before I was to load up the cargo van with two bikes, lots of Clif Bars, and an assortment of other necessities needed to get me across the country. Ninety days is a long time to be away from home, and if I could, I would have packed my own bed and refrigerator for comfort reasons. But unfortunately, neither would fit.

What was starting to worry me even more than what to take, however, was the cost of the trip in total. A half-dozen paid workers, van rental, gas, hotels, food—the dollar amount this baby was going to cost was getting scary since it was self-funded—and I was swallowing air pretty fast. I can assure you that the logical side of my brain was expressing great doubt about the whole thing, while the big picture side of my brain was quietly answering back:

It will all work out...you'll see.

The thought was exceptionally heavy on this July 18th evening as I had time to think. I was walking to pick up my bike after a final professional tune-up...getting ready to ante up to the pay counter one more time. I was thinking very hard...and questioning myself and the Universe...with a brutal third degree.

To myself:
Why do you do things like this, Shawn? What in the world are you thinking? This is going to be such a giant waste of money!

To the Universe:
Is this really what I'm supposed to do? Am I on the right page here?

Walking with head down and with much less than an optimistic mindset, I happened to walk right over the top of a very small, tightly wound up piece of paper shaped like a square. It looked like it could be a dollar bill. I bent over to pick it up.

I think I just found a dollar.

As I unfolded the corners, I realized that yes, it was money...but it wasn't a dollar.

Hmmm...I see a zero...I think it's a ten spot.

One more unraveling and I discovered I was wrong again. It was a one hundred dollar bill.

At the exact time I was worrying if the *Extra Mile America Tour* was the right thing to do...if I was spending too much money...I find a one hundred dollar bill.

Coincidence? Some would argue, "*Yes.*"

Interesting.

What do you think?

I'll tell you, with my head held high, and looking upward... with a renewed bounce in my step and a dramatic bolstering of my confidence...what I believed couldn't have been more clear.

EXTRA MILE HERO

The Human Element

...making a difference one kid at a time

When I met Regina Jackson during the Tour, she was coming straight from a sleepover. Now the mentioning of a sleepover would normally not be that big of a deal, but this event was special; it had hosted 150 sleeping-bag campers between the ages of six and eighteen. The previous night had been a fully charged evening complete with video games, movies, charades, arts, crafts, make-overs, nail polishing, and karaoke contests.

Oh yeah...and she had led the cooking of breakfast the next morning.

The second time I talked to Regina was on the phone after the Tour. This time, she had just come back from taking nine kids (ages fourteen to nineteen) for a whirlwind, sixty-hour trip to Washington, DC. On the trip, Regina's entourage stood on the steps of the Lincoln Memorial where Martin Luther King gave his "I Have a Dream" speech. They visited the White House, and they even had a private lunch with President Obama's sister. Most importantly, the kids got to imagine life outside of their Oakland, California, address.

You see, the kids that Regina Jackson has dedicated her life to come from a unique world completely foreign to the vast majority of us. These kids live in a neighborhood unflatteringly referred to as the "*Killer Corridor.*" In this thirty-block area, murder and assault exist at a higher rate than any other size-matching region in the United States. It is impossible to live in this part of Oakland and escape either hearing about or seeing something related to life's darkest side nearly every day.

If you live in this corner of the world, sleepovers are a special escape from reality…and going to Washington, D.C., doesn't even seem like a life possibility.

Regina Jackson makes them both happen.

In a world where so many of us try so hard to create the perfect existence…the perfect career, perfect bank account and perfect life partner…there is one person who goes into one of our country's most imperfect places with the hope of making it just a little better. That's Regina.

As Executive Director of ***East Oakland's Youth Development Center*** for the last fifteen years, Regina has poured her life into changing the future of the *Killer Corridor*. She does it by making an impact on one single child after another; she does it thousands of times over. Regina believes that if she touches enough of the kids who live there individually, then collectively the whole area will change.

Regina doesn't think small, does she?

If a kid from the local neighborhood wanders into the Center, Regina and her team immediately go to work to show them a whole new world of "*What if…?*" She brings new possibilities and experiences into their lives. She plants vision seeds. She guides and re-directs. She empowers. It is reasonable to assume that without her seed planting, many of the kids would have a future much shorter in days and breaths.

"*So often our young people don't get out of their own zip code. I want to change that. I want them to see that there is a world of possibility outside the ghetto.*"

How does she do it?

Regina commits 70 hours a week to developing free educational and employment programs for local kids. She builds creative programs in music and the arts. She has been instrumental in building an athletic department that keeps 1,200 local kids engaged annually. She helps young people find work. Regina Jackson is the ear when no other exists. She is the hugging arms that are there to comfort when others can't be found.

What do you tell a twelve-year-old who has witnessed someone being killed? What do you do to help an eight-year-old who comes from a world of parental drug use and abuse? How do you guide a teenager whose father has been in prison forever? These are the questions Regina answers daily.

Regina Jackson first teaches *Killer Corridor* children to cope and survive. And then she teaches them how to thrive. She does this every single day.

When kids are on safe emotional ground…they are taken to a higher level. The bar is raised, excellence is expected, and lives are changed. Regina knows how to give confidence. She allows kids to see beyond their own circumstances. She knows how to take a kid away from the wrong crowd and put him in line with the right crowd. Regina Jackson knows how to show up for kids who aren't used to people showing up for them. She believes in life-changing moments and helping kids find a more positive destiny.

When asked why she would put herself so far out on the line in such an uncomfortable world, Regina whips off a Marion Wright Edelman quote:

"Service is the rent we pay for living."

If you met Regina, you would recognize one of the most disarming and intelligent people ever. She is a leader and organizer extraordinaire who has the ability to work in society's highest paying jobs. But she doesn't. Instead, she chooses to utilize every inch of herself…and a 30,000 square foot facility in the heart of danger… to make an unselfish difference in life. She dedicates her life to bring "home" to the Hood. She never stops sharing the message that the young people of the *Killer Corridor* don't have to stay stuck in an address where hope currently shines dim.

"In some jobs when you give your best, you can never see how it resonates. Every day I can see what my effort does...and there is no better reward than feeling that."

At the end of my very first meeting with her, I asked Regina what her *extra mile wish* in life was. She answered:

"One day, I would like kids from the Killer Corridor to visit 1600 Pennsylvania Ave. Can you imagine these kids decorating a Christmas tree on the White House lawn?"

Although many of the stories about the kids she works with do not have a happy ending, we now know this one did. And yes... maybe those nine kids didn't get to DC in time to decorate the White House Christmas tree...but having lunch with a member of the First family isn't too bad, either.

Today, we seem to live in a world dominated by computers and technology. The human...face-to-face... element in all our communication is slowly being replaced. Regina reminds us that the power of humanity should never be replaced. Her life work reminds us that if we want to make a positive impact on a person's life destiny, the human element is everything.

Thank you for this reminder, Regina.

Thank you, too, for reminding us that true success in life is not about the size of one's paycheck...but the size of one's heart and commitment to pursuing good. In this, Regina undoubtedly shines as one of the wealthiest people I have ever met.

UH OH...NOW WHAT DO I DO?

The Tour was not short of uncomfortable challenges. It is easy to think that the physical test of riding all those miles, day-after-day, would be the hardest thing to do...but for me, it wasn't. Actually getting on the bike and pedaling was the one element of the *Extra Mile America Tour* that I could 100% do on my own. I had faith in me, and I knew I could push myself when I was tired. It might hurt, but I knew I could do it.

The other parts of the tour scared me more. In aspects regarding lining up cities, people, and support, I needed to rely on a team of people. I could only plan (and hope) that their efforts would be as passionate as mine.

Sometimes, I was lucky in accomplishing this goal. Sometimes I wasn't.

My ace in the hole was, "A.I." or "3.957." That's what I call Annika Ihnat. "3.957" has a UCLA graduating GPA of the same number, and everything that she did for the *Extra Mile America Tour* matched in quality and excellence. Annika was responsible for finding me the great *extra mile Americans* I spoke with in each of the twenty-one cities. She was also the one who worked hard to get twenty cities and two states to declare 11/1/09 "***Extra Mile Day.***" (Thank you, Hawaii and Arizona!)

My second "go to" person was Debra Amador...a creative water-walker out of San Francisco. She owns her own Public Relations firm, ***Mindful PR***, and takes on clients who "*get it*" and want to give back to the world more than they take. At first, I think I must not have "*gotten it*" with Debra because she turned down working with me. It was the first time in my life that I ever knew a vendor willing to walk away from money. Thankfully, after much convincing that I was worth her energy, she was finally persuaded to join the team.

Debra linked me up with the ***HandsOn Network*** offices across the country. The people of these amazing non-profit support organizations were key not only in providing individual city support, but also assisted in providing interview locations as I pedaled coast-to-coast. Debra was also responsible for lining up endorsements from the Mayors' offices along the route from San Francisco to Boston. Psychologically, her calls and e-mails gave me a huge boost up a few steep hills after hearing what she had accomplished.

A third person...unbelievable in her effort...was my wife, Christine. To say she was invaluable in contributing to the success of the Tour is an understatement. Initially, her major responsibilities included defining the daily bike route (which roads to take and how many miles to ride each day), but those duties soon blossomed into something much larger. Due to an inability of a hired gun public-relations professional to create "buzz" for the Tour, Christine jumped in and did what the pro couldn't do. She generated 90% of the over seventy media opportunities I had while on the road. Her dedication and persistence created many fantastic interview opportunities...each of which empowered my legs to keep going.

Unfortunately, though, not everybody measured up like these three in commitment and heart.

I had focused long and hard on finding the perfect road manager for the Tour. This was the person who would be with me every day driving the support vehicle...the one who would make sure I was covered as far as food and water...the one who would help me at events...the one I would rely on heavily to help me get across the country safely. This person was crucial. After going through a lot of applications and many referrals, I thought I had found the "*one.*" Always remember, though, if anything seems too perfect...run!

I failed to apply that lesson here.

It was my second night on the road, and I had just finished a great day meeting *extra-mile people* in Oakland when disaster struck. In the middle of the night, my road manager quit. The first two days were just too much for her, and she blasted me with her words, attitude, and demands. It was not a pretty picture.

Even worse than her verbal onslaught, she refused to go a single mile further driving the vehicle. Sacramento was a day's ride away. If she would crew for me for just one more day, I could get to Sacramento where I had the potential to re-group and find another support person. However, she wasn't going to help me get there…no way, no how. Despite being paid for the first 30 days in advance… she just flat out was not willing to *go the extra mile.* She left.

Uh oh…. I was in trouble big time and the whole Tour was now in crazy jeopardy on Day Two! Without a support person, I was pretty much buried.

What in the world am I going to do now?

In the middle of the night, I hit the phone. I needed help. Bad.

Here I was in a hotel in Oakland, California. It was midnight. I was stranded with a bike I needed to pedal and a support van that needed a driver. A tough eighty-mile ride was scheduled for the next day, and I was already wiped out physically from pedaling what little I already had. To top it off, I would now be riding on zero sleep.

My brain was spinning, wildly looking for solutions. Towing the van behind me just wasn't a good option. It was, however, a better option than one I was hearing. A few phone voices were suggesting that I consider postponing the Tour and getting off the bike altogether:

"*No one could blame you if you did.*"

At midnight…on Day Two of a ninety-day Tour…hearing

someone say you could quit is a very gut-wrenching message for a guy who has spent half a year planning.

There was one huge problem with that option, however. It just flat out didn't register with me as even being possible. In my world, "*quit*" is not a word I support. When I start something, I need to follow-through. It's melted into every fiber of my being. "*Don't quit…don't quit…don't quit!*" If I ever did quit, I would lose total belief in myself. My own goal integrity would suffer a fatal blow, and I knew that future goals would forever risk simply being "*wishes*" on a list. I believe when you give yourself permission to quit once, it is even easier to quit a second time. No…quitting was not going to happen now…and certainly not on something called the *Extra Mile America Tour*. I was just going to have to get through this and truly earn my *extra-mile stripes*.

In the case of the lost road manager at midnight…yes…I was facing a huge problem and my stress level undoubtedly had risen to a 10 out of 10. Never, however, did I have my finger on the escape button. I knew I had to find a way to keep going. I knew this problem could be solved, and I just had to piece a solution together step-by-step. I might not have been able to find a new road manager to carry me across the country in one night…but I didn't have to. I just needed to find someone to help me through the next day. That was it. That's all the moment really required. I could do that.

And I did.

Thankfully, two saviors came through for me…a family cousin, Laura…and a 67-year-old mother, who only six weeks prior had been in the hospital for seven days for major stomach surgery. Oh boy!

Laura got Mom down there, and Mom, tired and stressed, took over driving the van to Sacramento as I pedaled. Despite losing me for one ninety-minute long stretch as she searched for a Subway sandwich shop to feed her son, she did an outstanding job…and if you are ever looking for a road manger, I highly recommend her.

Living in Sacramento allowed me the chance to regroup.

Miraculously, on a Thursday afternoon, Christine was able to get the okay to take off work for two weeks. On Saturday morning, she jumped on board and took over driving the support vehicle for the next sixteen days giving me time to solve the permanent road manager dilemma. Of course, there would be numerous other challenges to overcome during the remainder of the Tour, but this was the granddaddy of them all. It was the life-and-death moment of my *Extra Mile America adventure.*

Phew!

My stress level rises again just recalling this story. Sometimes we are lucky the past is the past...aren't we? But now...truthfully...I can smile at the memory. I averted disaster. It may have been one of the hardest and longest 24-hour periods of my life, but I made it.

I've learned that if we can just find a way to keep standing in the cold storm for a little longer, the climate of our thoughts and feelings eventually begins to warm again. With the rise and fall of another day, a new sun never fails to turn a seemingly dark and dreary moment into one a bit more optimistic. It may take a lot of extra days...but eventually, hope again shines.

If we just hang in there.

Sometimes, it's super tough and painful to go through, I know... but if we can just find a way to keep going and have confidence in knowing that the combination of time and effort cures all...we will survive. And in surviving, always do we grow stronger, wiser, and more able the next time a storm enters our world.

And in my case, this time, when all was said and done, I earned those *extra-mile stripes.*

Journal Entry July 22:

Bad directions pedaling out of Oakland, and I got lost. Serious climb over the hills and over Grizzly Peak...hard day riding. But the real topper? At 11:45 P.M., Leah gave me an ultimatum: sign off on all my wishes or I'm leaving the ride. A midnight scramble with C.A. to cover options. Thankfully, Laura and Mom will come and bail me out tomorrow. No sleep tonight....

Journal Entry July 23:

...Mom and I headed off on a long day. We lost each other once, and I had left my darn cell phone in the van and had no way of getting a hold of her. Stupid. I sat out in the boonies... in 100 degree heat...out of water...exhausted...and totally stressed. I was sitting in the road with no shade thinking, "This really sucks...and I'm only on Day Three!" Finally, I thought something may have happened to Mom, so I started pedaling back adding even more miles to the day's ride. After about five miles, the white van came hauling down the road carrying a much needed sandwich. I was never so happy to see Mom in my whole life....

EXTRA MILE HERO

What Will You Be Doing For The Next 49 Years?
...the lessons of a 95-year-old

Instantly, I was taken with the way she focused on me as she approached. It was her turn to be interviewed, and it was my turn to chat with the 95-year-old, *extra mile*, wonder woman.

Raynia Kinniston was one of fifteen *extra mile Americans* I would be interviewing in Sacramento, and as I quickly scanned my notes about Raynia, I knew this lady was going to be someone special. Sure, being five years short of the magic *one hundred* had something to do with her uniqueness, but that's not why I was talking to her. No, she was here and had earned her place at the *extra mile table* because she had been volunteering at ***Mercy General Hospital*** for 49 years.

Uh huh...49 years.

Who in the world does that?

As I gathered my pre-interview thoughts, my brain spun through its collected "*What to do in the case you ever meet...*" file. I mean seriously...95 years old...49 years of volunteering...this woman was true *extra-mile royalty*. Coming up with no previous experience from which my brain could pull, I resorted to the mere basics: I smiled, extended my hand, and simply realized I was lucky to be sharing time talking about *extra mile stuff* with a person who had made a whole life of actually **doing** *extra mile stuff.*

With personality galore, Raynia took my hand in both of hers, looked me in the eye, and said:

"*I have looked forward to meeting you.*"

Ha! How funny! Raynia Kinniston had looked forward to meeting me? A master of positive first impressions, this lady either was gifted with the blood of a public relations pro…or she just really loved people.

It turned out to be the latter.

Bright as a whip, Raynia captured me not only with her keen mind and conversation, but most importantly with her *extra-mile story.* Yes…it was true...she had been volunteering at the hospital since 1960. And yes, it was also true, she had put in 47,000 documented hours of service in those 49 years.

But I needed more perspective. What did all these numbers really mean? As I listened, my pen scribbled some quick calculations on my notebook page.

"*That's 4,700 hours…divided by 8 hours a day…equals 5,875 work days.*" The math continued. "*There are 52 weeks in a calendar year…No way!…22!*"

My mental "*Wow!*" meter had hit the top bar. Raynia's volunteer work in hours was equivalent to more than 22 years of working at a full-time job!

"*Wow!*"

Even more incredible is the fact that Raynia is still at it. She still gets up three days a week and catches a 6:10 A.M. bus. She then hops on a connecting train in order to finish her hospital commute. From there, she plants herself in the hospital gift shop smiling and spreading good cheer.

Sure, it's easy to be impressed by the fact she is 95, has volunteered at the same hospital for 49 years, and is still going strong. We should all be so blessed. But what I found most impressive about Raynia was something entirely different. It wasn't her age or years of service. It was her story about why she chose Mercy Hospital.

You see, Raynia Kinniston ended up working so long and unselfishly at "*Mercy*" because she just flat out loves life. We all know hospitals are often considered the beginning…and often, too, the ending…of the most precious and beautiful of all gifts…life itself.

Raynia knows this. She has lived it.

At *Mercy General Hospital*, she has experienced life's happy moments at the highest of levels; her son and two grandchildren were born here. At this same hospital, Raynia also experienced life's most bitter and sad moments; this is where she was when she got the news that her son had died. Her husband, too. This hospital…this specific location…this special place where life begins and ends for so many was also the place where so many of her friends and neighbors had found their very best days…and their very worst days.

It all happened here. At *Mercy General Hospital.*

"*I just want to be here with people when they get their news. I just want to support people in what they are experiencing.*"

Being only at the beginning of touring across the country…on a bike…sharing the message of how great life can be when we have purpose and passion, I knew it was a blessing to meet this woman so early in my travels. This woman knew life. She knew how to treasure it and hold onto it with every fiber of her being.

And she knew how to help others do the same as well.

When my short time with Raynia was over, I knew it was in physical presence only. Down much deeper in me…in a spiritual sense…a seed had been watered. In the future, I would imagine Raynia's eyes smiling at me and her voice whispering to me:

"*Keep doing your best, Shawn…every day…all the time…until the end of your days.*"

P.S. Three months later after finishing my ride and returning home, I met Raynia again. After that second meeting, she sent me a card which is sitting right now on the coffee table in my home. The card reads, "I shall never forget you, Shawn." As you can imagine, it holds a super-special place in my heart.

Rest assured Raynia Kinniston, I will never forget you…or your life lesson…either.

EXTRA MILE HERO

One Determined Voice
...12,000 listeners

In 1999, Jody Ruggiero's daughter was in high school.

Like most parents, Jody juggled her worry time back then among all the never-ending influences that could sidetrack her teenager from fulfilling her potential: friends, alcohol, boys, drugs, and academic disinterest. Jody was also greatly concerned about what was going on inside the schools. Her concern led to action, and she ran for a seat on the school board.

And she won.

But it wasn't the work that Jody Ruggiero did on the school board that got attention or that qualifies her mention now. It was something that she did as a parent. It was something that she did to stand up for other parents in her community of Reno. It was something she did to bring awareness and connection back to families throughout northern Nevada.

The seeds were planted after she heard the news of what happened in another high school on April 20. Tragically, 1,060 miles away in Littleton, Colorado, two high school students armed themselves and went on a killing spree that took the lives of twelve classmates and a teacher in what was the deadliest high school shooting in United States history. Much of the early blame of this horrific event was directed at the Goth lifestyle of the two student killers and the music to which they were dedicated. Shock rocker Marilyn Manson took the biggest hit and much of the early finger-pointing responsibility for the tragedy.

Upon hearing that Manson was going to be coming soon to her town, Jody went on red alert. While she knew that Marilyn

Manson's music did not actually cause the murders at Columbine High School, it was clear to her that there was some connection between the shock rocker's violent lyrics and the troubled teens who perpetrated that horrific crime. She hit the phones and the fax machines. Personal calls to the Governor numbered 200. Personal calls to Reno's Sheriff Department numbered 125.

She was asked, "*Are you going to protest the event?*"

She answered, "*No. I am going to have it cancelled.*"

And it was.

Feeling the power of what one determined person can do, and believing that the Colorado shooting was a result of a great disconnect between parents and kids, Jody put her ability to think big and speak forcefully to work one more time. She vowed to do something for her community that brought kids and parents... families...together.

She created ***Tune In To Kids***.

Now seven years strong, *Tune In To Kids* is northern Nevada's biggest family day event. On one day each spring, over 12,000 family members come together to join in a day that celebrates reading, math, science, arts, culture, hobbies, health, and fitness. It is a day to remind parents all over northern Nevada that the success and health of their kids is up to them. It is a day to get kids away from the television and video games, and outside participating with the family. Undoubtedly, there are hundreds of kid groans at the "*Let's go!*" suggestion...but by day's end...family members are reunited through healthy activity and communication.

"*Parents need to understand their tremendous potential to influence their children in positive ways.*" Jody continues, "*If parents would just focus on less screen time and more real time, they would be shocked by the changes they would see.*"

Tune In To Kids started with one parent's loud voice...and her unwillingness to let go of something that bothered her. In life, we all often see things that bother us. In our hearts, we are struck with a biting anger because what we have just seen or experienced is wrong.

Too often, however, we do nothing. We complain privately, but never publicly. We are sideline sitters. We walk through life as mere witnesses and fail to stand up and let our voices be heard. We fail to take the lead and let our actions re-direct real change.

We end up suffering. And society ends up suffering.

Thank goodness, though, Jody Ruggiero is not one of those people.

Jody reminds us to live by the power of our convictions. She reminds us that one voice can make a difference. She reminds us that a family's success is directly related to a parent's commitment.

One person. One voice. Thousands of families. That's the Jody Ruggiero model.

And one we should remember the next time we are struck by the discomfort of seeing something that we feel is wrong.

CHIPPING OFF THE TAR

Can you imagine pedaling across the Nevada desert… **in August?**

Well, I can now.

Let me share five visuals of what it's like. I'll even throw in one small lesson Interstate 80 taught me.

Five Interstate 80 visuals:

1. There's lots of *bump…bump…bump…bump.* In certain stretches of Nevada's Interstate 80, there are miles of indented vibration lines in the emergency shoulder lanes. These are perfect for waking up sleeping drivers, but they play havoc with a bike rider's head. Pedal over too many of them and you start to feel like you are in danger of giving yourself a concussion.

2. The sun beats down with a vengeful mission. Also, depending on where the sun is in the sky, sunscreen or not, one side of your face develops a deeper tint of dark red than the other. Oh…and by the way…there are no trees. Finding shade? Oh…please!

3. There are lots of giant, plastic soda bottles thrown alongside the road. They are all partially filled…and, I assumed, not with the original contents. They seem to correspond nicely with the hundreds of empty beer cans that are also readily apparent. (A curious note about the beer cans one dodges along the road pedaling across the country: each state definitely has a beer drinking preference.)

4. It's lonely. Lonely, that is, until one of the giant trucks passes a few feet from you. When that happens, you hold

on to your bike handle bars super hard, keep focused on the road and prepare to be bounced a bit. After it passes, you say a prayer and wish for more loneliness.

5. There are lots of interesting artifacts along the road. In one small stretch, I happened to cross paths with a child's doll, a baseball bat, a variety of single shoes (although I did find one matching counterpart another mile further up the highway), a few music CD's, and even women's lingerie. No doubt each thrown-out-the-window article had a story on why it took flight, and when you are pedaling for eight hours in a day, you even start to imagine what some of those stories might be.

One Interstate 80 lesson:

Evidently, this was a summer when lots of road work was necessary. You know, the type of roadwork that produces unpleasant smelling black tar; the type where automobile tires pick up the tar particles and you can hear the small particles clinking off the underside of your car. Well…trust me…you have never experienced road work…really…unless you are on a bike and pedaling. My bike tires picked up the road tar so much that my bike gained pounds of weight.

Yes…pounds.

At first, you don't seem to notice as your sun-fazed thinking tells you: *It will all come off…just keep pedaling*. When the air is 100 degrees and you have nowhere to rest, you just don't want to get off your bike and check things out. So you don't.

But that's a problem.

The tar doesn't fall off. And when you try to scrape it off, it fights to stay on its new tire home. Finally, I had to pull over and use a metal bike tool to chip off the tar by hitting the tire at a strategic angle nearly as hard as I could. My arm action almost felt like I was attempting to chop wood…but with one hand. Stopping alongside the road every couple of miles to clean my tires became a nightmare.

But what choice did I really have? I couldn't pedal with it on; it had to come off. It was a serious test of will.

Pedal...pedal...pedal.

Chip...chip...chip.

Pedal...pedal...pedal.

Chip...chip...chip.

That was the routine. For miles.

But while I was out there...sweating and chipping...I was struck by a revelation. Call it sunstroke if you want, but my brain was communicating a valuable life lesson:

When life gets super hot and the pressure rises and anxiety climbs... when rest areas are non-existent and road tar impedes your progress... that's your chance. That's your chance to show that your goal really means something to you.

Realizing that small lesson...at that moment...not only got me through the rest of my tar removal pit-stops, but it carried me the necessary 73 miles from Lovelock to Winnemucca.

Journal Entry July 29:
...OMG! How big is this state? This road has no end it seems! I know I'll regret having written this later...but I sure look forward to the Rockies. The monotony of the Nevada scenery along I-80 starts to add up....

SOME DAYS IT'S HARD TO GET STARTED

Ever had a day where it's just hard to get started?

Some days on the Tour, just rolling out of bed and planting both feet on the ground seemed to be worthy of an Olympic medal. A seventy-mile uphill bike ride the previous day didn't secure a reason to bypass the ride of over seventy miles scheduled for the new day. Success on one day never gave me a free pass for the next. It just meant I had to start pedaling the day with legs already pooped.

The Tour certainly had its share of mornings when I felt I deserved a Gold Medal just for rising, no doubt. Often, however, the real challenge of any day has nothing to do with getting used to the morning sun; it is surviving everything that happens after the morning sun. Trials in a day can start to tumble over us like falling dominoes one after another when we get on a negative role...especially when our day starts with a flat tire.

In my case, on this particular August 7th, it started out with three flat tires. Uh, huh...three.

Bike mechanics is not my strength. In fact, *Bike Repair 101* is a subject in which I would probably rank last in the class. There are things in life that we know are our strengths...and then there are those topics we know cause our brain to go numb when we are required to participate. Bike repair, in general, is for me one of those brain-numbing topics.

And in particular...changing a flat tire.

Sure, there are those that may be saying:

"*Are you kidding? You don't know how to change a flat tire and you rode a bike across the US?*"

My answer to them is a stoic, "*Yep.*"

Knowing this trivial "*He is no bike mechanic*" fact about me is critical to the rest of this story. Because on this particular morning, basic bike repair skills were essential to getting me rolling out of the motel parking lot. Undoubtedly, you can imagine my complete disgust when I walked down to the van only to find bike #1 with dual flats.

Yes…both tires.

"Uh, oh!" (That's the G-rated version of what I really said.)

Quickly, however, I remembered my second bike and I soon felt a wave of relief. Smugly, I thought, *Well…this is why I have TWO bikes with me.*

After loading the *Green Hornet* back into the van (so named because of its color), I unloaded the Blue Pearl (aptly named because of its hue and with a bit of homage thrown to Johnny Depp's ship, *Black Pearl,* in *Pirates of the Caribbean*).

"*Uh, oh!*" again (this time muttered with even more disgust and fervor).

The second bike also had a flat.

Out came the bike pump and the patch equipment. Up went my blood pressure and anxiety. It was only seven in the morning, but I sensed that today was going to be legendary.

Go back to bed…and sleep…you need it. This was my brain solving the problem. *Get up later, and maybe then you'll remember how to do a tire repair.*

Our brains are great at giving us winning directions at times… aren't they? Sometimes we have to wonder if they are even on our side. But alas, I didn't go back to bed…and instead, I practiced my cuss words.

One good thing about struggling with a bike in a motel parking lot with lots of other guests loading and unloading suitcases in the morning is that you're bound to get attention. Sometimes in life, if you look like you're struggling just enough…with an occasional desperate foot stomp thrown in for attention…someone will be there to throw you a helping rope.

Today, I got one. On this morning, a couple from Australia... who just happened to be traveling with their bikes, too...were there to bail me out.

Jenn, the wife, came over first:

"Where you riding today?"

I shared the story of my in-progress cross-country adventure, and she was so excited about such a "*grand goal*" that she went back to her motel room to prod her Aussie husband out of bed. Phillip, not sure what all the fuss was about at first, got into his groove when he learned the topic was bikes. The sleepiness faded quickly from his face, and his Aussie tongue went into gear fast...making it possible for me to understand a solid 70% of what he said.

Upon discovering I was a total lost soul when it came to the whole bike tire repair thing, Phillip didn't hesitate a second. Down on the ground he went. I had my own Australian bike repair man at my service, and my day was back on track.

Despite Phillip making me nervous every time he unscrewed one of my tire's valve stem covers, followed by his Aussie brogue asking me, "*Do you know what to do with these?*" followed further by him tossing the cap blindly over his shoulder...he got the job done masterfully. Making sure to keep a close eye on the caps' landing zones in order to retrieve them later, I just nodded my head as if I was in agreement. Hey...I was getting my bike fixed, and who was I to argue?

Valve cap differences aside, Phillip got me up and rolling. Fast.

Actually, the rest of the day, I seemed to have just a bit more "*push in my pedal.*" I had shared time with a great world-traveling couple and was once again reminded of another simple "bike lesson."

No...not "*Learn how to repair a flat tire.*" Okay...maybe that lesson taken to heart would be helpful, too.

This lesson was something different. This lesson was a clear reminder that when you have one of those days when all the air in your day's tire goes flat, there is no need to call it quits.

Just call for help instead.

People want to help people; they really do. It's in our nature to help. On that August 7th day, two strangers again proved this by taking their time in helping me alleviate what could have been a pretty bad day.

I need to remember to help more. Maybe I won't be able to repay the kindness by helping someone else with their flat tire, but I can most certainly stop and ask a person with a map extended outward, "*Where are you going, friend?*"

Journal Entry August 7:

...Today was my lucky day! Both bikes were down with flats first thing in the morning. If it wasn't for Phillip and Jenn (bicyclists from Australia), I would still, no doubt, be sitting in the parking lot fixing my tires...

ONE HUNDRED MILES

I wanted to give it a shot.

I had never officially planned on it doing it, and I never even shared the goal, but in the back of my mind, I was always looking for that one part on the map to pedal **100 miles in a day**.

Having a goal of pedaling a 100 miles was certainly not one of the Tour's more noble goals. Admittedly, this one was 100% selfish. I did it to prove to myself I could. I did it to prove to myself that with heart, focus, and consistent action, I could conquer bicycling's famous century mark.

For me, pushing myself is an important part of my life. If I don't, I have a tendency to fall into a rut, do the norm, and eventually wonder where the days, weeks, and months went. I believe in keeping my ax sharpened mentally, emotionally, and physically, and the only way I know to do that is to step outside of my comfort zone every once in awhile and "feel the pain."

It's not just about exercising hard either.

More often than not, it's disappearing by myself with a notebook and evaluating how things are going in my life. It's asking myself the hard questions and taking an honest look at why things might or might not be happening.

Long ago, I adopted the maxim:

"If it's going to be, it's up to me."

Pushing myself extra hard every once in awhile…in a number of areas…sharpens my ax for great accomplishment on the days that follow.

The funny thing with me, when I push myself physically, is that I become tougher in all areas. Think about it. When you are exercising hard, it takes mental and emotional will. It takes the ability to push past your brain shouting: *Stop!*

In pushing past that crucial keep-going point, however, I have found that positive things happen: my creativity flows, my attitude becomes more empowered, my confidence in my ability to do big things intensifies.

When I get to the "quitting point" and somehow find the strength to push past it...I always win physically, mentally, and emotionally. The hardest part, though, is convincing myself of this fact when I am closing in on a spot where the decision "*to go or not to go*" begins weighing on my mind.

On this particular day—during my ride of 100 miles—I recited a mantra over and over:

"*Ride like the wind. Ride like the wind. Ride like the wind.*"

This positive affirmation pushed me faster than normal without "feeling" the miles. They just kept ticking off...*11...23 ...45...63...77*...comfortably.

But as I got closer to the century goal, the exceptionally hot August day began to take its toll. When I stopped for breathers, I made sure they were short breaks. I didn't want my brain to begin kicking in anything contrary to what I was purposefully planting in my head. Sometimes, our brains do that.

"*Nice job! You've gone far enough for the day! It's too hot to pedal any more. You can stop now!*" is not conducive to going the distance.

Often for me, I find that if I take my foot off the "gas pedal," I potentially open the door to running out of energy...and will...and I don't make it to my pre-determined goal. At the 77 mile mark, I consciously made the decision that this was not going to happen today. I had gone too far not to give it a shot.

"*I'm going for it!*"

Although this 100-miles-in-a-day goal was all about me, I needed to eventually involve other people in helping me cross the

Grand Junction, Colorado, finishing line. And...oddly enough... none of these people I knew, but I needed to rely on their energy completely.

As my ability to prod myself forward began to fade, I started to do something a bit unusual perhaps...but it was all in fun and goodwill. I started waving to every single big-rig truck driver that was approaching me from the opposite direction. I found if I started my across-the-highway wave soon enough, truckers would see me and blow their big truck horns in a big "*Hello!*" back at me. Like a kid, I never got tired of playing the "wave-horn" road game, and the positive energy I began to feel from their big truck horn blasts undoubtedly took my mind off my worn-out legs and body.

So to all of you big rig Interstate-80 rollers, I want to thank you. Thank you for not only pushing your goods through that hot Nevada/Utah/Colorado desert, but thank you, too, for making it possible for one 46-year-old, tired cyclist to achieve a personal goal for a day.

I might have created the goal...and had the desire to make it happen...but on this day, I needed the help of a hundred eighteen-wheeler friends I had never met to get me to the finish line.

EXTRA MILE HERO

So Others May Live
...a mom's life-saving decision

Imagine if one day, your sixteen-year-old high school kid comes home from school and says:

"*Mom, if anything should ever happen to me, I hope that you would let them take whatever organs they can use to help someone else.*"

Imagine three weeks later if that same requesting child...died.

A dramatic theme in a script writer's tear-jerking imagination? No. Sadly, it is the real life story of a Utah mom named Lisa Osmond.

"*When I arrived in Salt Lake at LDS Hospital with Adam from Life Flight, he was evaluated, and then I was brought into the room where the doctor told me that Adam had been pronounced brain dead. The doctor explained what brain death meant and that it was irreversible. He truly was dead, even though he looked like he was asleep.*

"*I took in every last minute with my precious boy; loved and kissed him, and just sat by his side and smelled his hair. I just couldn't wrap my mind around the fact that he was never coming back home with me. I'll never forget the complete and overwhelming heartbreak that I felt at that moment. It was absolutely suffocating.*"

In early October of 2003, Adam Osmond made his request without even the slightest indication that tragedy was mere days away. In the days following that ominous October 23rd day, Lisa and her family followed through and honored Adam's wishes by having his liver, kidney, eyes, and various other tissues donated.

Undoubtedly, it was a horrific time that no parent should ever have to live through.

"The doctor asked me what I knew about organ donation, and I immediately had a memory flash in my mind. Three weeks earlier Adam had come home from his health class. He had come into the kitchen and was so excited to tell me that he had signed up that day to be an organ donor. I remembered Adam's desire...and I kept my promise.

"As soon as that doctor asked me about organ donation, I about jumped at him and said, 'Yes, Adam is an organ donor...you take him!' Despite the total loss that I felt, I had hope! Hope, that if my son wasn't ever going to come back home, at least he could save someone else. He would live on in others.

"After about three weeks, I received a letter in the mail stating that Adam was able to save four lives the day he passed away. He also gave sight to two different blind people. Plus, being a tissue donor, he improved many, many lives."

But the story doesn't end here. Lisa went the *extra mile.*

After surviving the worst day...and subsequent days of her life...Lisa had a choice. She could choose to live forever in bitterness at the cruelty of the Universe's decision to take Adam, or she could continue to live and make her life count.

Lisa Osmond took the worst day in the history of her world, and turned it into something that would have benefit and value to others. Remembering Adam's unselfish, life-giving request to have his organs donated, Lisa linked up with an organ donor registry called ***Yes Utah!***

In doing so, four great things happened:

1) She multiplied Adam's passionate request by seeking out other potential donors.

2) She added purpose to her life by becoming a difference-making spokesperson.

3) She became an advocate for continuing to live... despite death.

4) She became a model for overcoming great challenge.

Today, Lisa Osmond is one of Utah's leading public relations volunteers on the importance of donor registration. She gives presentations to schools and service clubs. She signs up new donors. She is on the front line of turning one person's tragedy into another person's blessing.

"Adam's liver recipient is a fifty-four-year-old gentleman, Steve Bird, who was on the verge of death. We were able to meet him one year after his transplant and, now, he and his family are part of my family. We have been blessed beyond measure in our healing by not only sharing Adam's story, but by educating the public on this amazing program."

That's a miracle of the heart…isn't it?

Who knows how we would respond if faced with the same sort of life-shattering moment. Hopefully, none of us ever will have to face the same degree of "horrible" that Lisa and her family faced. It is 99.9% certain, however, that we will each face an event in life that challenges us to rebuild after a moment of devastation. It could be a lost job, a foreclosed home, a bankrupt business, a heart breaking divorce…it could be a hundred different things.

When our time comes…and life delivers our "*Rise from the ashes!*" challenge…how will we respond? Maybe when our individual times do come, our spirits will be given fortitude by remembering an amazingly strong, tomorrow-looking woman named Lisa Osmond…and her son, Adam.

P.S. Lisa shared with me a few common facts about organ and tissue donation that would be good for all of us to know as we contemplate that individual choice for ourselves.

1. One organ donor can save the lives of nine people.

2. A single eye and tissue donor can restore sight to two people and improve the lives of up to 100 different people.

3. You can be a donor from birth up to age 80.

UNWANTED PASSENGERS!

Cerro Pass is an amazingly beautiful mountain pass in the Rockies. Breathtaking in its picturesque beauty, this pass is probably better enjoyed looking with awe out a car window at the scenery… rather than grimacing directly at the ground in front of you, grunting, at every passing inch of the road.

This particular mountain climb took a couple of painful hours, and it seemed as if my bike and I were only communicating successfully in one gear—the granny gear.

Two Things About The Granny Gear:

1. Remembering it from days as a kid, it's the gear you shift down to, as far as you can…the super easy gear.
2. Up until this point in the ride, I had refused to ever use it. By using it, I felt I was saying to myself, "The ride won't get any tougher than this!" Unsure if that statement was true or not, I felt a bit more confident if one more ace remained up my sleeve…in this case a gear on my bike… to conquer the future challenge.

Cerro Pass…regardless of what lay ahead in mountain climbing…became the point where I first used my granny gear and shifted down as low as I could. Tired legs…and the *now*…took precedence over mental poppycock…and the *tomorrow*.

Eventually, after climbing four grueling miles, I made it to the elevation peak of Cerro Pass.

After reaching the summit, I began riding down the backside. One to two miles per hour soon gave way to twenty-five to thirty miles per hour. I was still shaking from being so tired after the last push up the mountain, but I didn't want to get off my bike to rest once my speed began to pick up. Flying straight downhill now, the cool air blowing against my drenched clothes felt great! Still, I focused steadily on the road now quickly passing by...looking for stray rocks, pot holes, road cracks, or any other road hazard that has a way of quickly materializing and taking down a bicyclist.

And then I felt one. And then another.

"*What the heck?*"

A third...a sixth...a tenth one hit me! I was being attacked by road grasshoppers who were hitchhiking down the hill. After the fourth big green insect stuck to my leg, I started to get a bit creeped out. I began looking down the hill for a place to safely pull over and get out of the traffic, to rescue myself from the attack.

Before arriving at a safe spot, however, my legs became covered with grasshoppers! The rest of the way down the backside of Cerro Pass, I ended up stopping more times than when going up the hill...just to shake off my unwanted passengers.

Sometimes in life...when things seem all downhill and success should be easy...we get hit by life's grasshoppers. These are the unwanted day-to-day passengers that seem to think it is their mission to impede our success...and often, the quality of our days. Unwanted passengers seem to have a different focus and purpose than our own. They seem to think it's okay to hitch their emotions and efforts to our successful forward progress. It could be in words, attitudes, or actions...but there is no doubt that they make getting to our destinations much harder than necessary.

The next time you are cruising along smoothly...rejoicing in victory over your own successful uphill climb...don't let a few unwanted passengers bother you. Get off your bike only long enough to deal with them and flick them off.

And always remember, you're bigger than they are.

COINCIDENCE?

At an elevation of 11,312 feet, Monarch Pass was the highest point I reached on my cross-country tour. In retrospect, all the other mountain passes I climbed seemed like lion cubs compared to this roaring King of the Rockies. Situated high between the towns of Gunnison and Salida, Colorado, Monarch is a ten-mile climb that can make a grown man cry with desperate elation once the top is in sight.

I know. Because I did.

By the time I finally made the top of that monster climb on my bike, I was absolutely spent. Monarch Pass had demanded every single ounce of my will and energy. Mentally, I was exhausted from pleading with myself to keep pushing...using every single positive affirmation in my memory. I could barely talk.

Emotionally, I was in a mixed world between elation and desperate fatigue...the combined result being numbness. Physically, I couldn't walk but a few steps before I needed to sit...and collapse. Spiritually, I could only look skyward with a grateful heart that the climb was over and I had triumphantly survived.

Sometimes in life, it takes every bit of effort and discipline we have to keep going...to keep moving forward. Reaching the summit of Monarch Pass was one of those times for me. I had wanted to quit a hundred times. I wanted to say that *half* was good enough.

I never did.

Sure, I could have thrown my bike in the van and just watched the scenery out the passenger window. I could have bypassed hours of heart pounding delirium and cramping legs...but I didn't.

Sometimes, we just have to suck it up, hang in there, and keep pushing. We know if we do, the result will be sweet.

I found the sweet result.

Certainly, the physical feat alone will always stand out near the top of my "*I did it!*" list. Truth is, up to this point in my life, it was the hardest physical thing I ever did. This was my version of my own one-person, one-event Iron Man competition, and it is planted forever in my conscious to pull out when I need to focus on a "*You did it!*" moment.

This may not be true for you, but when I give a goal everything I have, I am rewarded by something extra that I didn't even expect. And that "something" turns out to be pretty cool.

I don't consider myself a religious person, but do consider myself a deeply spiritual guy. I look around me and know there is a reason for everything. What it is may not be clear exactly, but I believe there is a higher power in the Universe that helps me give it my all going up the mountains in my life. At various important times in life, I have been touched by that small coincidence that I have never really thought of as being a coincidence. And the perfect coincidence turns into the perfect gift at the perfect time.

On the day of my Monarch climb, I was to experience a "coincidence."

And a gift.

Moments after reaching the 11,312 foot peak at Monarch Pass, I sat down outside the Visitor's Center only to hear someone ask, "*Are you him?*" I was too tired to consider the question may have been directed at me. Heck, as far as I was concerned, this was a faraway land where no one knew my name.

The shadow of a person was looming over me, and I heard the voice again. "*Excuse me...are you the Extra Mile Man?*"

In disbelief, I looked up. Seeing a kind face looking at me, I took the moment in. "*Yes. I am.*"

Two days prior, I had been fortunate to have had my picture and story on the front page of a Montrose, Colorado newspaper. Today, I was being told by a Eugene, Oregon traveler that the story had inspired her and her husband. The story had encouraged them to vow to get their own bikes out when they returned home and start riding again.

The incident might have seemed very ordinary to some, but to a completely fatigued bicyclist who had just climbed into the clouds…who was riding across America to hopefully inspire others to *go the extra mile* in life…to me, this moment was a blessing of the highest proportions. It was a blessing of spirit. It was a blessing that took my temporary brokenness and restored every inch and fiber of my six-foot frame with a single goodwill greeting.

Totally soaked with perspiration, I snapped a few pictures with my enthusiastic encouragers. They had been the right people. I had arrived at the right moment. Nothing in the world would have warmed my purpose and passion any more. At that moment, I was experiencing the right everything. It was a coincidence that only a twinkling eye looking down on me from the Universe could have ever known I needed.

EXTRA MILE HERO

Camp Hobé

...a place where kids can be kids

Prostate. Lung. Colon. Kidney. Liver. Breast. Skin. Ovaries. Pancreas. Thyroid. Brain. Bone. Tissue. Uterus. Blood. Stomach.

It seems to have no limits to where it will go. And everywhere it does go, it has one mission: to destroy.

A doctor's pained words, "*I'm sorry...you have cancer,*" has touched a majority of families. Both of my parents heard the words. One out of four deaths in the United States is attributed to it. My father died from it.

The National Cancer Institute estimates that each person who dies from this ugly monster loses an estimated 15.5 years of life. That's a lot of years unlived...isn't it? Think of all the amazing things you would miss experiencing, if your life was cut short by fifteen years.

How about if you were to miss out on sixty years? High school, college, marriage, career, kids, vacations, friends...you would lose out on so much living.

That's what happens to a child who succumbs to this deadly disease; they lose a lifetime.

A child with cancer? It's hard to imagine many things in life's horror book more dark and sad. Just looking at a child's face... so much hope...so many years still to live...and yet inside his or her body, a disease is working so horribly quick with a mission of sucking the very last breath of life away.

Ugly. Horrible.

But cancer doesn't just work overtime trying to steal a kid's life. First, it seeks to wreak havoc on a kid's childhood. Often, it forces a child to quit being associated with all things kid-like. No more running and jumping without restraint. No more cannonball jumps into the swimming pool. No more running through the hills looking for lizards. Growth is stunted. Confidence is depleted. Isolation moves in. For a child with cancer, the physical, psychological, and social impact can be brutal. For a kid to lose the ability to be a kid? That's a smile-stealer from everybody's face.

But in Utah, fifty minutes outside of Salt Lake City, there is a special group of people…mostly all volunteers…who are dedicated to creating an environment where kids with cancer can go and smile. Since 1985, Utah volunteers have worked to create a place where kids with cancer can ride a bike, sleep in cabins with friends, shoot an arrow, hike…and even swim. They created an experience where these kids can be normal for a week without feeling left out. They created ***Camp Hobé***.

While interviewing people in Salt Lake City, I was introduced to *Camp Hobé* and taught much about the real life existence of a kid living with cancer. Christina Beckwith and Nicole Bailey, two *Camp Hobé* heroes, shared with me about this bright shining light in the cancer world. Compassionate beyond measure, they are both front line players in creating smiles where few exist…Christina as the Executive Director and Nicole as the Arts and Crafts Director. And although these two were my educators on the child cancer subject, they represented a whole legion of like-minded heroes who care deeply about these special kids.

Camp Hobé is a summer camp geared one hundred percent to kids with cancer, and to their siblings who are often forgotten in the family-cancer experience. It is a place where parents can feel safe in knowing that their child will be secure medically, and yet at the same time, be awarded with all the great privileges of a normal summer camp. It is a place where kids can temporarily forget the seriousness of the disease which their bodies carry, and they can be allowed to do things just like healthy kids.

At *Camp Hobé*, the facilities are amazing and everything is taken care of by the volunteers. There is a main lodge and seventeen cabins. Recreational facilities have been built that include an outdoor pavilion, swimming pool, an arts and crafts cabin, and a sand pit volleyball court. Oncology-trained pediatric nurses and a pediatric physician staff the on-site infirmary. People who love games and activities…and life…make up the other volunteer staff. For one week in the summer, all of these people dedicate their lives to giving two hundred kids a more normal summer week of childhood.

Camp Hobé kids are allowed to play outside with other children. They are given an opportunity to make lifelong friends of peers with whom they can relate and who are also living with the devastating disease. They are allowed to feel peace, be independent, and build confidence in a natural setting, away from the confines of a hospital. They are free from their isolation. They can escape worry about the future and facing their grown-up realities. For one week a year, the mission is simple: ***Give kids the chance to be kids.***

As I look back at my own childhood, I remember riding my bike to the park to break home run records with my neighborhood friends. I remember basketball at school recess and playing golf with my father in the early evenings. I remember holding hands with Laura Streng during games of Red Rover in the fourth grade. I remember walking to school and throwing snowballs during the winter.

Undoubtedly, you have a few sweet childhood memories of your own.

But kids with cancer? Their life experiences lead to memories far different…and less sweet. Except for *Camp Hobé* kids. For one week a year, cancer is not allowed to steal the fun and spotlight. Cancer is not allowed to take their childhood away.

Thank goodness for places like *Camp Hobé*. Thank goodness for people like Christina and Nicole. They recognize one of the great cosmic injustices and have vowed to do something about it. They may not be curing cancer, but they are doing something equally important. They are making kids forget they have it.

We all pray that some day a cure will be found for a word as scary in the English language as any there is. But until a cure is found, places like *Camp Hobé* that plant smiles for a week are life savers.

THAT DAY!

We have all had a "*THAT Day.*"

THAT is a day on our schedule...usually set for us long in advance...which we look forward to with a jaded eye. It is the ominously looming date when something is supposed to happen. It could be a planned holiday visit to the in-laws, the last day of a job, the day a huge presentation is required, the first day of a class...you get the idea. It's not necessarily a given that a THAT Day is a dreaded occurrence in our lives, but it is a day about which uncertainty and doubt cause our brain to keep reminding us of the turning calendar pages...and its upcoming presence.

August 17th in Denver, Colorado, was THAT Day for me. It would be on THAT Day a new road manager would join me.

Ever since Sacramento, my wife Christine had been handling all duties of the tour with complete excellence. Having been a part of my life for nearly 30 years, she knew how to meet every need that I required. On the tour, the van was where it needed to be when it needed to be there. She knew how hard I could push and when I should take a break. Her preparations were top notch, and she handled actual event days with precise organization and professionalism. She made just about everything in my days easier.

It would be a tough day to let her go and bring someone else in, but after August 17, she had to head back home, back to work and to her own life. Her replacement for the rest of the tour was flying in, and I wasn't looking forward to the transition.

For two weeks prior to her departure, I had been working the phones from the road looking for her replacement. Christine had been forced to jump on the tour and take over after the Oakland debacle in which road manager #1 had quit on the spot and left me stranded. Now, on August 17, Christine and my feeling of security were definitely out…and an unknown and great uncertainty was being let in.

Gotta' love days like THAT. Oh, man.

The new guy was Julian Walter, a highly recommended choice by Annika, my "A+" overall Tour Manger. The fact that the recommendation came from her gave me a little confidence, but still, I didn't know Julian and my original choice out of San Francisco had also come with stellar references. I was still rolling the dice.

Here we go again! Optimism was not coloring my thoughts.

Unlike most hires I have made in my life, this time I didn't have the luxury of re-grouping after a bad decision. This person had to roll with me every day for the next two and a half months. If it proved to be a bad choice…again…I was in serious trouble.

The very first day with the new guy was also to be a push for me personally. It was scheduled to be a ride of 92 miles, so I was nervous all the way around. With a pre-six A.M. start, I hoped to alleviate potential problems by getting rolling early. Julian survived the first wake-up call.

The energy was high for both of us as we got going. Julian seemed to want to do a great job, and I wanted to be an encouraging voice for him. It seemed like it might be a good combination.

But then our first challenge surfaced.

Requiring a moment of rest after pedaling against a ferocious morning headwind, I jumped in the passenger seat of the van. Because of the strong winds and the possibility that my bike would be knocked over, I avoided resting my bike against the van's side like I normally did. Instead, I parked it in front of the van.

After sharing with Julian that there was a great picture opportunity behind us that had been missed—"*C'mon…let me show you!*"—he started up the van to turn around and head back down the road. But as we attempted to go forward, we ran into a snag. The van's front tires started to spin in the mud, and we weren't moving. Julian hit the gas a little harder. More spinning.

My thoughts began racing: *Had Julian pulled too far over on the shoulder and gotten us stuck on his first day? Hmmm....*

My brain was twirling with possibilities as Julian shifted down and prepared to give it another big push.

"*Wait! The bike!*" I shouted.

The van wasn't going anywhere because it had knocked the bike over, and now, the van's right front tire was on top of the fallen bike... stuck. As Julian backed the van up and I jumped out, I was prepared to see a big, distorted pile of bike junk. With a disbelieving...and no doubt scared Julian jumping out of the van too, we assessed the damage. Amazingly, just a small bit of messing with the alignment and brakes and everything was fine. On day one together, we had just experienced a miracle. The pedaling would continue.

In the end, Julian proved to be an excellent choice. Being a professional photographer, he captured the tour beautifully from Denver to Boston with over 5,000 photos; he also provided great solo assistance on 15 event days. Together, we survived THAT Day, and his presence made a lot of the other days on the trip pretty great.

"*THAT Day*" will always be a part of our world. It will come... and it will go...and it will come again. Strong preparation... mentally and emotionally...is all we can really do to make THAT Day come and go smoothly.

And I have now learned it's best to tackle THAT Day with an attitude of positive expectation...and...maybe...just maybe...a sense of adventure.

Journal Entry August 18:
Can you believe it? On day one, Julian ran over the bike! LOL No worries. It all worked out well, and I nailed the 92 miles. The end of the day, however, was a real race. The sky grew terribly dark and from a distance, I could see the storm and lightening closing in. The last fifteen miles of the day I kept looking over my shoulder watching the menacing storm clouds chase me. The adrenaline carried my legs to pedal as fast as they could go.

GOOD PEOPLE

They're all around us.

Sometimes, we forget to notice them because for some odd reason, the media chooses to focus more on their counterparts. But if we look closely, we can identify them. They are the ones who say, "*Have a nice day,*"...and look at you straight on when they say it. They are the ones who take the time to show concern to a stranger in distress. They are the ones who share a smile everywhere they go.

I call them the "*Good People.*"

It's not as if they are an alien group from another planet... although with the infrequency with which we find them, you would think they might be. They are the ones who keep their promises. They are the ones who volunteer a lending hand. They are the ones who choose to mention the good qualities about a fellow worker being maligned by others at the water cooler.

"Good People" make the world feel...well...good. When we run into one, our own spark of "good" is ignited into something brighter. Negative thoughts are overshadowed, and we are even prone to pick up the "Good Person" mantle and pass forward the feeling that has been generated inside of us. "Good" often snowballs from "Good People."

When you ride a bike across the country, you create the opportunity to meet lots of people. Pedaling the United States is somewhat of an unusual activity, and people are often drawn to hear your story. It also seems the more we put ourselves "out there" in life, the more apt we are to run into "Good People." I guess when you're looking lost, tired, sweaty and hungry, that's a homing beacon for "Good People" to come to your rescue or just to do something completely *extra mile*.

On the Tour, I met hundreds of "Good People." Each, no doubt, would deserve mention here if I could. However, there were two back-to-back days in the state of Nebraska that particularly stand out.

Before I go on, I need to say that in my opinion, the Midwest grows not only miles and miles of corn...they grow thousands and thousands of "Good People." In the smaller towns, the chase for material gain takes a major back seat to the pursuit of being honorable and decent. "Kindness" catapults to the front of the line over self-serving attitudes and selfishness. If you've never ventured to the heart of the country...take a visit sometime and enjoy what I call a "Good People" vacation.

Now back to the story...

Imagine racing to get to the only store in a very, very small town, and when you arrive, you find that it is closed. But wait! The assistant manager of the store happens to be outside in her car preparing to leave for the day...and notices you. She takes the time to get out and ask if you would like to get something. She then opens the store just for you.

Imagine chatting with this same person at the check-out and asking for directions to the town motel. You learn the bad news that the motel is no longer in business and mentally and emotionally, you immediately begin to play another episode of "*Now what?*"

But wait...again!

The store assistant manager also runs a Bed and Breakfast...and although she wasn't planning on having guests for awhile...she invites you to spend the night. And then she says:

"*Pay me whatever you can.*"

That's "Good People." That's Valerie Rogers, assistant manager of the ***Stratton Country Market*** and owner of the ***Blue Colonial Bed and Breakfast*** located out in the Nebraska countryside. (And when I mean countryside...believe it! We had to wait for the cows to clear the driveway as we drove up to the house.)

Again, back to the story…

On a second entirely different occasion, imagine walking into a small town motel and chatting with the desk clerk. She learns about your *extra-mile*, cross-country story and feels so moved by your mission that she starts to cry:

"*I am inspired that you would do something like this.*"

She then shares her own story and what she has gone through… thanks you for your inspiration…and since her family owns the motel, she refuses to accept any money for the room.

That's a "Good People," too. That's Jayme Schroeder and her family owns the ***Plains Motel*** in Holdredge, Nebraska.

Valerie and Jayme…and thousands of "Good People" like them…surround us in life. They really are everywhere; we just have to keep our eyes and ears open. If you happen to run into one of them, consider yourself very lucky; they will undoubtedly add to your day. Better yet, if one of the "Good People" happens to be your friend, count yourself blessed by the Universe; they will add much value to your life.

And best yet, if you just happen to be one of the "Good People," you are probably one the of the richest people in the world in all things that money cannot buy.

Journal Entry August 20:

I have never seen so many stars in my life! Looking up at the Nebraska sky is one of the most beautiful and inspiring sites I have ever seen.

EXTRA MILE HERO

Finding Success

...the kind that matters most

When I first met this unique husband and wife team in Denver, I quickly appreciated the great respect that they showed each other. The way they looked at each other...always showing deference to the other...always smiling when the other person spoke...it really struck me. If any two people on earth were meant to find each other, it was this inspirational duo, Brad and Libby Birky.

As I listened to their amazing story, I was reminded of what can happen when a "team" rallies around the same concept. Even though this was a team of two, each member was solidly behind the other. Each was on the same page in belief, purpose, and passion. With a force like this, the Birky's together could accomplish whatever they chose.

They chose to open a restaurant...the ***S.A.M.E. Cafe.***

First, Brad quit his job in the computer world. Libby then followed leaving the classroom. Their 401K was cashed out. They walked away from financial security...risking everything.

But that's what you do when you have a dream bigger than your own comfort. And the Birkys did. They had a big, big dream. They wanted to cook and serve healthy food. They wanted to make people feel good. They wanted to open a restaurant.

Now opening up a restaurant is a fantastic entrepreneurial undertaking, but by itself, there is nothing earth shattering about doing so. Restaurants are everywhere.

Yet, Brad and Libby's restaurant would be different.

There were to be no prices on the menu. None!

This, of course, did not mean that customers would be met by a ghastly surprise after receiving a bill at the end of the meal. Quite the opposite. Customers would be met by receiving no bill at all.

At the *S.A.M.E. Cafe*, you pay what you can afford.

Yes, that's right. You are charged nothing. You simply have to look within yourself...and pay what you can. You see, the vision is to serve great tasting, freshly made from scratch, healthy food to all people...regardless of an ability to pay. This would be a restaurant for all to enjoy. It would be a restaurant geared SO ALL MAY EAT.

Generally speaking, everyone is still asked to chip in something. However, for those who have no money at all, they are still welcomed wholeheartedly. If someone can't pay anything for a meal, he or she has options such as cleaning tables, sweeping up, or washing dishes. This way, everyone who eats feels that he or she earned a place at the table. Everyone contributes something.

Please understand, though, this is not a restaurant designated specifically for those with little money. It's a place for everybody... and everybody comes. Families, business people...and those without jobs. The *S.A.M.E. Cafe* is a place for those struggling and for those not struggling.

It's for all of Denver.

In 2010, Brad and Libby will reach year #4 of operation, and they project to serve lunch to over 200 people five days a week. Normally for a restaurant to have that kind of crowd, it would mean a sure ticket to success at the bank. But this inspirational twosome still walks into each day not knowing what the cash register will bring. They also walk into each day knowing in their hearts and minds that they are making a difference far greater than any amount of money could ever measure.

The Birkys took a dream...and they went for it. No excuses in the world for these two...just vision, action, and faith. They stretched their minds 100% and flat out went for a goal far bigger than I could have conceptualized would ever succeed. But now...for them...success! Perhaps not success of the "*I am rich!*" kind...but definitely success of the "*I am leaving footprints!*" kind.

And that kind of success should really make us stop and think.

Because at the end of life...theirs, yours, and mine...which kind of success do you really think matters most when we realize our last breath is about to be taken?

I GO TO ALL THE CHURCHES

Divisions in opinion seem to be everywhere now...don't they? Every opinion-giver seems to be under the impression that his or her opinion has been blessed by the hand of the ultimate Decision Maker, and is, therefore, correct.

Some have an "*I know it to be true*" opinion on politics and the ills that are hurting one party or another. Others have resolute conviction on why the stock market goes up and down or what is needed to rebuild the economy. Others have little doubt why sporting team "A" will hammer sporting team "B." While still others just flat out seem to be quite willing to shout out judgment on the fact that you are living YOUR life all wrong.

With opinions on every topic floating around the world easily captured by some Internet source somewhere, it makes it pretty easy for us to come up with some of our own opinions. Just a little cut-and-paste here...add a little passion...and bingo! We fit right in, too.

But have you ever considered that maybe with so many differing opinions existing in the world that we have lost our notion that we really are all on the same team? This "*I am right! He is wrong!*" mentality really shatters the basic premise that we are all human beings sharing an amazing experience called "life" at the same address in the Universe called "earth."

We really do have something special in common.

But it is ignored.

It seems that opinions expressed with fire matter so much more. With such angry diversity existing everywhere, it really makes you wonder if true "peace and goodwill on earth" will ever be found?

I will save you from my opinion.

However, I will tell you about a motel manager in Hastings, Nebraska. His name is Vidu Patel. He is Hindu. But he goes to Christian churches. In fact, he is unafraid to go to any of the churches…all with an open heart. In fact, he looks forward to it.

Vidu doesn't push his spiritual beliefs...although his spirituality is obviously the most important thing in his life. He just looks at things differently and doesn't profess to have a monopoly on the truth. Instead, he wants to learn from you. He wants to know what you believe…not so he can lash out with a questioning tongue, but rather to expand his own knowledge and experience. He does not believe that he is right…or that you are right. He believes that there is room for all opposing sides to be right.

Can you imagine what would happen in Washington, DC, if Vidu was allowed to address both Democrats and Republicans in Congress for a day? How about if he visited the United Nations? How about if he just sat in each of our homes?

Maybe agreement would be a bit easier to find.

"*I go to all the churches and say my prayers*," says this humble, quiet, and sensitive man.

I am glad I remember Vidu now. He reminds me that I, too, need to go into all the metaphorical churches…and conversations… in my world with kindness and respect. He also reminds me that when I walk in, everybody might smile a bit more if I just leave my opinion outside the door.

NOT TODAY!

August 26th started badly from the very beginning.

When you're riding a bicycle, one of the least pleasant things to do in the world is to ride in the rain. On this particular day, I was greeted by rain in its most menacing form. You know the type… the sort of rain that figuratively feels like there are one million water hoses in the clouds turned on full blast. Upon waking, I heard the dual combination of pounding rain and cracks of thunder. It was clear from minute one that today was not going to be a bike riding joy.

Nervously peeking out from behind the hotel curtains, it was obvious that this storm would capture the day's entire agenda. The morning's dark gray sky was regularly igniting with bolts of bright light, and after each bright light…a giant "*Boom!*" Mother Nature was not a happy camper.

Now if I had a choice, I would never have even gotten on my bike in weather so bad…but today, there was no doubt what I had to do. My Omaha event was the next day and I still had a lot of miles to go to get there. Regardless of what I REALLY wanted to do, I knew I had to tough it out and pedal; I had to get the miles done. I began to prepare myself mentally for a long day.

As I pulled my bike out of the van and started pedaling, the whole day had a feel of "*This is impossible!*" to it. It wasn't just raining, it was pouring. After only twenty minutes, I could not have been any wetter if I had jumped in the local Platte River. My shoes and socks were soaked to the max. My feet were ice cold. The back of my rain jacket was covered from neck to lower back with mud from my rear tire kicking road wetness up at me. I was not having a good day.

But still, I continued.

Finally, with Omaha closing in and requiring just a couple of more determined hours of pedaling, I stopped at a fast food restaurant one last time just to dry off. I picked up a cookie inside so as not to feel guilty for using their paper towels and drying myself off a bit with the hand dryer in the bathroom. I ate the cookie as slowly as I could and watched the rain come down…hoping…praying…for a two-hour weather reprieve.

Have you ever had a premonition? Have you ever felt that eerie, ominous feeling that you should just hold back and not continue? I had one now.

It was easy to rationalize at the time that my brain just wanted me to call-it-a-day and make up the miles tomorrow after the event… but I didn't like to pedal "catch-up" miles. As I sat there slowly chewing each chocolate chip, I felt the need to pick up the phone and call a few people back home who had been emotionally helping me out every day. Was it unusual to call and say "*Thank you*"? No. But it was odd to feel a need to do so now. I made the calls with a quiet, foreboding energy. Obviously the rain had dampened my spirit.

Right?

In retrospect, we can always look back at disasters and see signs. I was about to have a near fatal disaster, and it was preceded by one giant sign…an ominous feeling inside me.

But still, on this day, I did not listen. I continued to ride.

Finally finding the power to get out the door and into the downpour one more time, I struggled to put my bottom back on the bike seat. But I did it. Once again, I was on the road…riding… with one last determination to push through to my day's destiny.

Then, ten miles further up the road, it happened.

I was going about sixteen miles per hour along the Highway 6 road shoulder when a giant pothole jumped up on me quickly. Realizing crash disaster was inevitable if I continued over the hole, I quickly jerked the handlebars left in an attempt to guide my bike's direction into the regular car lane. However, there was a problem with that. Besides the pothole, there was a ledge a couple of inches high between the shoulder I was currently riding and the highway lane I was trying to get onto. As I turned my bike to go over the ledge, my bike tire hit it at a bad angle. My front tire slid along the inside ledge line instead of jumping over it. I didn't make it into the car lane.

Correction. My bike didn't make it into the car lane.

In a nanosecond, it all happened. I went flying over the top of my bike and onto the wet highway. The force and direction of my catapulting body sent me tumbling not just through one car lane, but it took me into the second. With my head now lying horizontally on the road, I could see a car racing toward me doing 55 miles per hour. I saw the car tire swerve quickly and miss my head by a couple of feet. Luckily, too, the driver in the next car saw the situation and was able to hit her wet brakes and swerve without hitting me either. As more cars came speeding my direction on this dark and rainy day, my brain...as dizzy as I was at that moment...went into rescue mode.

Get up...get off the road, Shawn! Now!

I pushed myself to my knees. With my body aching and my skin stinging beyond belief, I crawled to the shoulder. Then I collapsed.

The first driver, Robin, whose great driving skills saved her from hitting me, pulled over and came to my rescue. Five or six cars in total had stopped to make sure I was okay. Thankfully, I was.

I didn't want an ambulance called, but I did need help getting to my support vehicle which was waiting farther up the highway. My front tire had turned awkwardly the opposite direction and, at that moment, my bike was in no shape to transport me further. Leaving my bike by the side of the highway, I got into Robin's car, and she drove me up the road to where Julian and my support vehicle were waiting.

After connecting with Julian and re-telling the story, I carefully examined my physical condition. Deep road abrasions stung my knees and knuckles. Both were bleeding badly. My shoulder and side hurt from the crash landing, but nothing was broken.

We drove ahead to an overpass where we could turn the van around and head back down the other side of the highway to retrieve my bike.

After a couple of miles heading back in the opposite direction, I saw my bike from across the highway.

"*There!*" I pointed over at the scene of the accident.

Finding the next overpass, we exited the highway, then got back on again going in the direction of my crash. Finally, we saw my bike and pulled over to give its damage an evaluation.

Julian started to load the bike so we could head to Urgent Care when I said:

"*Hold on. I can't go to Urgent Care yet, Julian. I need to finish.*"

In disbelief, Julian stared at me as if I were kidding.

"*I'm okay…the hospital can wait. I only have about five miles to go to finish the day's ride. I need to get back on my bike…now…today …so I won't be scared to get back on it later.*"

And that's what I did. I finished the ride.

As I rode the last few miles, I felt very afraid of slipping again. Every pedal stroke I took was slow and deliberate. My deeply scraped knees stung viciously; blood was dripping down my leg all the way to my socks. But still, I rode…focusing even more intently on every inch of the road ahead of me.

Within about fifteen minutes of beginning to pedal, I felt an intense wave of emotion sweep through me as if I had been given the ability to "feel" for the very first time. The potentially fatal seriousness of my accident hit me unexpectedly and with a rush. I started to cry.

I was crying…not because of the physical hurt I was feeling… but because I felt grateful I had survived. As I replayed my brain's recording of the incident in my head, I realized how lucky I had been. The timing for my accident had been perfect. There had been no car immediately next to me, and the driver who dodged me was paying complete attention to the road. Everything had been perfect in allowing me to walk away with the least amount of damage to myself as possible. At that moment, I knew I had dodged disaster… and disaster had dodged me. The Universe had given me a reprieve. Today would NOT be my day to go.

After the incident, I was asked by a few people in my intimate circle why I didn't go to Urgent Care immediately. I didn't because I knew if I had gotten off the bike, I would have allowed fear to carve a place in my spirit that was as deep as the abrasions on my knees. I knew that the more time that I let pass before getting on the bike again, the more fearful I would be to ever get back on the bike. When you are riding a bike across the country, being afraid to get on it is a pretty big deal.

That happens, you know. We get afraid. And then we quit.

We let failures…small and big…dominate our thoughts. They eventually become so strong, they prevent us from continuing. We begin to focus on "falling off." We begin to visualize crashing. We are reminded of how our "knees" felt with road burn…and that it could easily happen again.

When we begin to focus too much on all the possible "horrible" that can happen…we end up eliminating all the possible "great" that could happen, too. We deal ourselves the ultimate "*Not again!*" card, and we stop trying altogether.

We quit "riding."

Success in life has so much to do with psychology…our own. Eventual success always depends on what we let our minds dwell upon:

a) the pain of previous failures, or

b) the enormous satisfaction we will feel when we do successfully make it to the finish line.

On this particular August 26th day, I had to get back on the bike. I had a choice…but in my mind…the choice was obvious. I was not going to sabotage myself. I was not going to feel scared to go again tomorrow…or the next day…or the next day.

There was no way in the world I was going to let myself… defeat myself.

EXTRA MILE HERO

BIG Dreamers

...bringing Love, Hope and Strength to the world

Some people really dream big in life, don't they? Maybe you know one or two of them. These are the folks for whom just dreaming of a new career or planning a cruise doesn't cut it. They want far more. They want to go after really BIG goals.

Some BIG dreamers seem to have a different fear level meter built into their nervous system than the rest of us. Little scares them when it comes to setting their goals. Dreams that would cause most of us to be filled with the red-alert sort of adrenalin that says, "*No way, Jose!*" cause a rare few to be filled with a burning, "*Gotta' do it!*" desire.

Some brave souls desire to perform in front of hundreds. Some people want to visit exotic countries. Some people want to climb the world's highest mountains. Some want to develop fund-raising events to help others.

While the goal activities listed above cause most of us to hit the brakes, there are those few who lick their lips with a special relish as they consider the possibility. Nervous anxiety is non-existent. What does exist is red-fire passion.

There is also a THIRD group of people. This group looks at the above goal list and doesn't think about picking one of them to go after; they think of going after ALL of them.

Simultaneously.

The ***Love Hope Strength Foundation***, headquartered in Denver, Colorado, is an organization that includes people who do things in this order:

1) They climb the world's highest mountains,
2) perform fundraising rock concerts at these locations, and
3) use the money raised to provide much needed medical equipment for cancer centers around the world.

That's dreaming with a sense of adventure. That's dreaming with a world vision...with a higher purpose. That's dreaming BIG.

In its first two years, the *Love Hope Strength Foundation* has performed music concerts on six continents. Talk about fast starts. They have led musical pilgrimages to remote venues such as Mount Everest base camp, the top of the Empire State Building, the Inca ruins of Machu Picchu, and the Mount Kilimanjaro glacier. They have found some home-based grounding, too, by conducting bone marrow drives at the largest music festivals in the United States. Their efforts are flat out saving lives…here, there…everywhere.

Part of the *Love Hope Strength* cancer army is made up of musicians from every corner of the globe. Legends in rock n' roll from groups such as *The Cult, The Stray Cats, Gin Blossoms,* and *The Fixx* have jumped in to climb…and perform. Nepalese folk singers, high school bands…musicians from all over the world participate and join in the musical effort to help cancer victims.

How are they making a difference?

They purchased the first mammography and internal radiation machines for the country of Nepal. They funded a mobile cancer unit in Peru capable of screening 30,000 patients a year. They funded a new wing at a cancer care center in Wales. They are sharing the advances made in cancer care and sending supplies to cancer centers in need around the world.

How did a vision like this start?

In 2007, *Love Hope Strength Foundation* was co-founded by leukemia survivors Mike Peters of the Welsh rock band *The Alarm* and entertainment executive James Chippendale. They wanted to find a way that people everywhere had access to the special resources that could save their lives. It's all pretty impressive.

I learned about this inspiring, big dreaming organization from its charismatic day-to-day leader and coordinator, Shannon Foley. When Shannon talks about where they are going, it doesn't seem like a big deal...to her. But when she talks about helping cancer people around the world? That's her big deal. The climbing...and the rest? That's just the unique spin to help cancer patients...and have a bit of fun in life at the same time.

Having purpose can be fun, too. And it can be inspiring.

People talk all the time. They talk about what they're "*going to accomplish.*" They talk about all the great goals they are going to achieve. They talk about writing the book, going back to school, going on safari, or starting a business. And as so often happens...all the talking leads to little action.

Love Hope Strength Foundation represents the opposite. They don't just talk. They do. And they do BIG...very, very big.

The kind of dreaming Shannon and company does? That kind of dreaming I admire. The kind of action they take? That I admire even more.

JUST WALKING THROUGH

Walking through cemeteries is not something I ever did before I got on a bike to pedal across the country. Sure, I have been to Arlington Cemetery in Washington, DC, a couple of times, but only because it is on the tourist map of "*Must see!*" sights and is a respectful and encouraged activity. Besides walking up to see the Tomb of the Unknown Soldier and John F. Kennedy's Eternal Flame at Arlington, however, cemetery sightseeing has never been an activity for which I signed up.

On the *Extra Mile America Tour*, however, this all changed.

It all began as I entered the Midwest just east of Colorado. On the smaller country roads I was pedaling, I started noticing the isolated, seemingly abandoned cemeteries. At first, I just took a mental note that they were there. I noticed the old fences surrounding them. I noticed the sometimes decaying and falling arched entry gates. I noticed from a distance the seemingly different and dramatic headstones. After passing several over the course of a couple hundred miles, curiosity began to strike.

I walked through one.

As I stepped in between and around the extremely weathered and often hard-to-read grave markers, I noticed that all of "life's permanent retirees" now in residence had been gone for decades. Some had even been gone for close to two hundred years! There were no recent "move-ins," just tens and tens of old-timers.

Walking through, I began to get a sense of history. I imagined the events that were going on in this country at the time. I imagined what their lives must have been like…how they made their living, what experiences they might have had.

And as I contemplated their history, I couldn't help but begin to think about my own history. Someday in the very FAR future, I pray, chances are excellent that both you I will take up permanent residency in a place like this. Although chances are pretty darn good we won't be sharing a unit next to "*Robert Smith 1806-1871*," we will become a part of the life cycle that eventually embraces us all.

In life, we all share the fact that we have a beginning and an ending date. My cemetery walk-throughs gave conclusive evidence of this universal truth. Furthermore, there is nothing we can do about those specific dates. They will be what they will be... regardless. And although our eventual marker might highlight those two days in history specifically, each of our individual lives will represent so much more. Our lives...and our history...will be represented by everything we do *in between those two dates*. And for all of those in-between days, we are in control of how they will be written.

Standing before a grave, I would find myself wondering about the details of the man, woman, or child who had been laid there. I wondered about their stories. Realizing at 46 the odds are pretty good I have lived more of my years than I have left, I think about my legacy and what difference on this earth I might make.

"Will my life have mattered?"

It is a big question to contemplate.

I discovered that it is good to take a walk through a cemetery occasionally. It is good to be reminded that this amazing gift called "life" is not forever. It is also good to contemplate the "*Will I matter?*" question...while we still can make a difference.

Journal Entry September 1:
I stopped in one of the small cemeteries today and walked through. I noticed lots of couples buried together. On one stone, there were the words "United Forever"...and a carved picture of two rings interlocked. They had each other forever... what a sweet thought.

STRESS FREE ZONES

If you ever decide to go for a Sunday bike ride, ride in Illinois.

After having competed with car and truck traffic for lane space halfway across America, it was a welcomed blessing to have the chance to pedal hundreds of miles without worrying about the fast moving car coming up from behind. I didn't have to worry about having only a six inch road shoulder—or no shoulder at all—on which to pedal.

I didn't have to worry about giant big rigs barreling down on me…or even worse…the stock truck "leakage" that came from hauling pigs and cows. I didn't have to worry about drivers who had a mission of letting me know the roads were not meant for bikes…nor did I have to worry about objects thrown my direction. And not once did I have to worry about that occasional spitter.

Sure, I had to ride for twenty, thirty, forty miles at a time without road support…but it was worth it. When it came to spending time on the non-motorized bike roads of Illinois, I was smiling. All the time.

I could finally just relax…and breathe stress free.

Illinois has non-motorized vehicle and pedestrian roads like the *Hennepin Canal Parkway State Trail*, the *I & M Canal Heritage Park Trail*, and the *Old Plank Road Trail*. And they are amazing. They are simple trail roads…sometimes dirt, sometimes gravel…a bicyclist can use to navigate across the state right through the heart of nature. When you are on one of these trails, cars seem a hundred miles away…and so do all the worries that civilization brings.

Sometimes the trails are more suited for *mountain bikes,* where the water has washed out the path, but that only adds to the Lewis and Clark-like adventure. You simply pick up your *road bike* and haul it off trail through the trees until you are able to reconnect with the good road.

The roads follow man-made water canals over ninety years old, so the ups and downs of the path are minimal. The ride is mostly flat and there is no hard pedaling…just easy, enjoy-the-scenery pedaling.

You are alone, away from everything. They are stress free zones.

Have you ever noticed how nature can be a mind cleanser? Have you ever felt the refreshing nature of being in…nature? When I am out there, it feels like I learn to breathe all over again. Quick, short breaths are replaced by long, deep breaths. It seems I can feel my forehead lines release a bit, too. In nature, life is simplified; complications are removed. The need for checking e-mail is gone. Life without a cell phone signal? It's hard at first, but…Wow!…is it ever freeing. The busyness of everything moving so fast around you takes a backseat to watching a butterfly flutter slowly in the air.

On the *Hennepin Canal Trail*, trees grow thick and natural. When they see you, turtles slide off of the rocks and splash into the water. Deer graze fearlessly. Frogs playfully jump about. It's a refreshing break from the deadlines, bills, and pressing urgency my everyday world so regularly presents.

Riding on the *Hennepin Canal Trail* was a perfect reminder of how good it feels to make time to simplify life. I need to do it more often. Spending a day at a sporting event or going shopping? Nahhh…not the same sort of relaxation release. What if my team loses? What about that ugly charge showing up on my credit card statement at the end of the month?

We seem to have created lots of great opportunities to relax in order to cope with life's stress. And maybe a few man-made experiences have an ability to let us release a little steam from our ever boiling life. But I'll tell you, nothing in my experience has ever felt as good as that occasional day off just to walk, hike, or bike through nature's escape.

Ahhh…the *Hennepin Canal Trail.* I wish I were riding there now. Maybe on a Sunday in the future, I'll head back to Illinois to enjoy nature's stress free zone.

Journal Entry September 4:
…Turtles were everywhere today. I came across one flat-shelled guy who was out sunning on the road. He seemed a little slow, and I didn't want something to find him and make him supper, so I picked the little guy up, walked him back to the water, and watched him speed away. If nothing else, I saved him from a long walk back home.

EXTRA MILE HERO

Spellbinding Moments

...we're never too old to leave our deepest footprint

I love a good story. Perhaps you do, too.

You know the kind; it makes a book nearly impossible to put down despite pressing obligations.

"*Dinner's ready!*"

"*Be right there!*"

Twenty minutes later, with nose still in book, you press onward without having made it to the dinner table...absolutely needing to know what's going to happen in the next chapter.

Storytelling doesn't always have to be delivered through a good pen either. It can be shared by a person to a group verbally. Sometimes, in fact, when the storyteller is really good, the story can take on even more color...especially for kids. Think back to an early grade school teacher who just seemed to make a story even more magical as she told it.

I remember sitting in class as a little guy...spellbound...as the teacher captivated me with her storytelling creativity. We students bounced up and down, shouting out when she erred in reviving the voice of a familiar character. We would remind the teacher loudly, "That's not the right voice!"

Germaine Dietsch is a person who remembers how life-impacting that special spellbinding moment can be. As a child, her favorite stories were those told by her grandmother from memory and from the heart. She remembered the excitement of listening as a child. When she became an adult, Germaine recognized the feel-good moment and sense of value it created for the storyteller... especially one in his or her senior seasons. In fact, she recalled the benefits for both parties...senior storyteller and junior listener. It was so significant that she created an organization which brought both child and senior together regularly in a storytelling capacity.

She created ***Spellbinders***.

Each year *Spellbinders* reaches out to an audience of nearly 300,000 children in over 2,000 classrooms, libraries and other venues. They have trained over 1,200 storytelling volunteers, and now have chapters around the country, as well as in Canada and Wales.

Spreading storytelling magic, that special senior and child interaction is recreated over and over again. *Spellbinders* do not read to children; they tell stories in the ancient world tradition. The folk tales and legends, most of which predate print and have been passed through the ages orally, are learned—not memorized word for word—by the volunteers. *Spellbinders* tell their stories eye-to-eye and heart-to-heart.

In the late 1980s, Germaine started to feel that there was a serious disconnect between the old and the young. The young were not reaping the wisdom of the old...and the old were not capturing the vitality of the young. In a storytelling setting, this would all be changed. Remembering how in the ancient past a community would gather around a fire in order to listen to the sage advice of an elder, Germaine decided to take a lesson from yesteryear's storybook and re-create the same storytelling setting and experience. Imagination would again be sparked; community would be re-established. The old would enthrall the young by telling a story.

For the child listener, creative thinking would be engaged. Imagination would be nurtured. For the older storyteller, a sense of self-worth would be re-established. Mental and emotional health would be improved. It was a complete "win-win." With *Spellbinders*, an age-old tradition of spellbinding storytelling would be re-established, and both parties would reap life-changing rewards.

Today, *Spellbinders* trains individuals, mostly over the age of sixty, to become magnificent storytellers. It then places these unique individuals as volunteer storytellers in schools. The volunteers develop a relationship with their "kids" as they continually return to the same classes to tell stories throughout the year. Connection is established.

In a society where technology and the media seem to cater to a younger and younger crowd, it is easy to start feeling out-of-date.

"*I'm too old to do that!*"

"*At my age? Are you kidding?*"

People like Germaine Dietsch don't listen to conservative "hold back" thinking. Germaine was 51 when she embarked on a Masters Program. She was 56 when she started *Spellbinders*. At 78, she is as active and as committed to creating as ever.

People like Germaine refuse to listen to the whispers surrounding us that tell us we are "*too old*." Age is a number…and if you want to feel old…go ahead; you have that option.

But you also have another option.

With chronological age, wisdom and experience grow. And with wisdom and experience, we each have the opportunity to create our biggest life footprint to-date. Sure, we can turn the page with each fading year and say, "*I remember when….*"

Or we can choose to prop ourselves up at the center of life, learn to tell a great story, and eventually experience our greatest joys and success. And maybe…just maybe…in telling a story and creating opportunity once again, we may discover ourselves in the center of a group of kids, mesmerizing them with our words, and feeling more alive than ever before.

THIS, TOO, SHALL PASS

I stood in front of Abraham Lincoln's statue in Ottawa, Illinois. It is a taller-than-life monument capturing a legendary man who has become a giant in our history's truth and imagination. Directly behind Lincoln, was the statue of another historical statesman. It captured the held-in-time likeness of then incumbent United States Senator Stephen Douglas listening to Mr. Lincoln, shown in an oratorical pose.

In the center of this small town is the park where, in 1858, Lincoln and Douglas held the first of their seven famous debates on whether "*All men truly are created equal.*"

As I stood leaning on my bike in front of the statues of the two men standing tall and timeless, I was captured by the fact that over 150 years ago, ten thousand people stood on this same ground listening to them debate. This crowd had come miles to hear these two dominating political leaders debate on the great issue of their time.

I closed my eyes and imagined.

As I pedaled across the country, historical road markers along the way made a perfect resting spot for my weary legs. I could recharge my body and simultaneously review some history lessons. I was lucky. Going slowly on a bike certainly made regular pit-stops more convenient than if I had been in a car.

With life moving so fast today, especially in the seemingly daily advances in technology, society's focus appears to be constantly on the future: "What about tomorrow?" As much as anybody, I am forward looking, yet I still appreciate that there is much to be learned from history…and sometimes…it helps to remember it.

It is also easy to be captured in the drama of the present. Undoubtedly, each of us has experienced an occasional dark period when the light switch to our world seems impossible to be found. When this happens, we forget how to smile and life becomes an uphill struggle. We get out-of-whack emotionally and life seems hard, bitter, and hopeless. We can become so caught up with the anxiety of the "now" that we forget that no bad moment lasts forever, and that there will come a time…soon…when we again can laugh and enjoy life.

Standing at this historical site, I could only guess the anger and intensity of the crowd's emotional state. At that time, the issue of slavery was an enormously heated topic. It became a life-and-death fight for not only hundreds of thousands…but for our entire country. Bypassing any of the social lessons that can be learned from the moment, I chose, instead, to focus on another lesson I am learning as I age:

"***In time, things are resolved.***"

In learning to take that simple thought into each challenging moment, I cope better throughout the troubling period. When I fully embrace the truth that "*Nothing lasts forever,*" and "*This, too, shall pass,*" the seriousness of the trial I am currently experiencing appears in better perspective.

And that's a good thing.

Like the powerful Lincoln-Douglas memorial commemorating that famous day in history, we too have our own pivotal moments.

And if we reflect enough on the lessons of our own life, we will discover that we have succeeded in surviving the tough moments.

During our toughest times, perhaps it is best to not look to the future and conjure up what might happen. Perhaps it is far healthier to look at the past so that we can be reunited with the simple truth that "***This, too, shall pass.***"

EXTRA MILE HERO

The Flying Nurse
...saving lives from the air

Some little kids want to grow up to be firefighters, presidents, or ballerinas. Others look deep into their imagination and believe they can be professional athletes, singers, or television stars. Still, others think about being doctors or nurses.

Teresa Elder fell into the latter group.

When she was a little girl, she carried around a junior medical bag. In middle school, she became a Candy Striper at the local hospital. And when Teresa Elder grew up, she became what she dreamed of. Today, Teresa is a life-saving nurse.

Now, to me, all nurses in this world are special. It takes years of hard work, dedication and discipline to acquire their valuable "*I am a nurse*" classification. It takes a great brain to learn all those long words and then know what to do when someone has an ailment represented by one of those words. But most of all, nurses seem to be blessed with an extra dose of giant-sized compassion.

And that makes the rest of us lucky.

Nurses are the ones who linger by our sick beds, give us confidence, and make us smile. They are the ones whose words seem to soften the reality of where we are. They might have been initial strangers...but often...for that brief moment when we have to meet them professionally, they can become our greatest friends.

So even after establishing the fact that nurses are a special group entirely, I cast a vote that Teresa Elder stands out as EXTRA special. In her very humble manner, she would quietly debate this point, "*But I am sorry, Teresa...you are.*"

First, Teresa works in a setting far more unique than her hospital-bound peers. In fact, she works above the ground. That's right...she works in the air. Teresa is in a helicopter most of the time. Oh yeah...and sometimes she is even on the side of a mountain.

Teresa Elder is the Chief Flight Nurse for ***Flight For Life*** in Colorado.

She is the adventure nurse.

Founded by Denver's St. Anthony's Hospital in 1972, *Flight For Life* became the first hospital-based medical helicopter program in the United States. Today, this "go to the victim" organization responds to life-threatening emergencies in hard to reach places in nine states. They assist in search and rescue operations, ski and hiking accidents, and avalanche rescues. *Flight For Life* is the pioneer in the field of air medical transport, and since their initial flight nearly forty years ago, over 300 flight programs around the world have been modeled after them.

Available twenty-four hours a day, *Flight For Life* is there... waiting...for that emergency call from a physician, an ambulance service, a fire department, a law enforcement agency, a ski patrol, or a search and rescue group. And when that call comes, Teresa...and nurses like her...unhesitatingly jump into the helicopter without question. Each call leads to a unique landing spot. Each call leads to a victim's best chance of surviving.

No pressure, huh?

Gulp!

Within five minutes of receiving a call, Teresa and her team (her, the pilot, and a paramedic) are up and in the air coming to the rescue. I consider them the Medical Calvary, and hopefully, they will turn out to be the best part of someone's very horrible day.

Can you imagine what it must be like to get the call? As the nurse (a nurse is the lead medical expert on board), Teresa is heading into an environment with limited equipment...just what she can carry in...and what the helicopter has on board. Her team's goals? Resuscitate. Stabilize. Transport.

Her team just wants the victim to have a chance at life, and they do their best to get a victim to a hospital where a more extensive medical team waits with all the gadgets. Each year, *Flight For Life* records some 4,000 emergency lift-offs. That's 4,000 potential accidents...and emergencies...whose victims' chances of survival increase greatly when Teresa and company take to the air.

Recently, a patient of Teresa's had a full cardiac arrest as they closed the helicopter's doors and became airborne. Oh boy...talk about a potential panic moment. She didn't. She saved him.

There are lots of special stories.

Once, a woman had been riding her ATV in the mountains and had a bad accident. The helicopter flew in and landed as closely as it could to the victim on a mountain ridge. Able to grab only a medical bag, Teresa started the challenging hike down to the woman. When she arrived, Teresa found the woman unconscious, with a severe head injury, and very close to taking her final breaths. With no other medical support or gear, Teresa inserted a breathing tube and hooked up an I.V. She hunted through the nearby tress, found a couple of old boards, and with the victim's friends, carried her down the mountainside to a meadow where the helicopter could land. The woman's life was saved.

Now that's a "day at the office" a bit different than most of us experience...isn't it?

I remember a song from my younger days, "Mommas, don't let your babies to grow up to be cowboys." Well...really...why not? Why not continue to feed the dreams of young kids for as long as we can. Because every once in awhile...like with Teresa...one of those special kids...with his or her special dream...might grow up and do something super special...like really save the world.

Walt Disney said, "*If you can dream it, you can do it.*"

And if that really happened...if that childhood dream did come true...the world would probably be the biggest beneficiary. The fulfilled dream might cause many to smile. Or sometimes, the fulfilled dream might help a few lucky people to live another day.

AND THEN THERE WAS LIGHT

Nothing can undo a guy's sense of security more than... getting lost.

We are all quite aware of the running jokes about men choosing to do anything BUT ask for directions:

"I'm not lost! I know where I am going!"

I'm not quite sure what that's all about, but maybe someday... after I find myself...I will dare to delve into the topic of why most men refuse to honor the authority of a map, or even stop and ask for help.

On the bike trip, I can assure you there was no bravado about using my own sense of direction. I flat-out have a terrible sense of direction, and if I didn't live near the Pacific Ocean, I would never even know where west is. On my cross-country bike venture, map reading...and map following...was an integral part of everyday life. On a bicycle, a "pedalist" has much less flexibility when he misses a turn and goes ten miles the wrong direction. On a bike, an error of misdirection eats up both time and energy...physical and emotional. Both time and energy are precious commodities when you have to pedal seventy miles in a day.

For the most part, the *Extra Mile America* team nailed the route pretty well. We dissected every day's ride with numerous resources, always with two goals in mind:

1) get me there, and, 2) find a safe road.

The first was always easier to do than the second.

In seeking safe roads, we looked for the secondary road least traveled. In states where non-motorized roads existed, I wholeheartedly jumped on them...and loved it.

Except for TWO days.

On those two days…map or not…I got lost.

Now getting lost would normally not seem like the potential end-of-the-world when you have a working cell phone. Even on a bike. Most of the time, I could pick up a phone and dial:

"*Hey, Julian…where are you?*"

But sometimes, even having a phone connection was not enough.

The first time I got lost was on the *I & M Canal Heritage Park Trail* in Illinois. I had only encountered Julian twice all day. The trail I was pedaling had few connection points with the motorized road, and Julian and I would take advantage of every meet-up point we could find. Sometimes, however, the map just didn't seem to jive with reality.

This was one of the days.

It was dusk and the sun had already left the sky. I was ready to call it a day and thought I was at the last meet-up spot.

Shawn: "*Hey, Julian…I'm here. Where are you?*"

Julian: "*I'm here, too.…Where are you?*"

As it would turn out…we were not at the same place. Furthermore, it made more sense for me to pedal to the next hopeful spot rather than to wait for him to find a spot already proving to be deceptive.

I kept riding.

And the light kept waning.

And then it was totally dark.

And then I was pedaling blind.

And then bugs started hitting me in the face in groups of what felt like ten at a time.

And then I had to stop batting them away for fear of riding with one hand and hitting a giant root.

And then my bike kept bouncing over invisible dips in the trail.

And then I squeezed the handle grips as tightly as I could.

The "and thens" kept coming.

Noises were everywhere around me…and I couldn't see what was making any of them.

I had to start singing so the noises would hear my bad singing and think: *We'd better not fool with whatever that is!*

And then there was light.

In the pitch black of the night…a miracle! The bright beam of a flashlight peeked through the trees. It was Julian. He had stumbled onto the dark trail and found me.

Phew!

When the path seems ever so dark…don't give up. Hold on tight. Do what you can not to crash. Keep the monsters along the road at bay. Don't let a few mosquitoes cause you to lose control.

And then…keep praying for the light.

Because eventually it will shine. Sooner or later, it always finds you.

EXTRA MILE HERO

The Small Things Don't Bother Me Anymore
...putting life into perspective

On Wednesday, June 13th, 2001, Jason Jolkowski disappeared from his own driveway without a trace. The nineteen-year-old has never been found. Nor has a single clue to the cause of his disappearance.

There had been no sign that fateful day would be any different than any previous day in the Jolkowski world. Mom and Dad were at work. Jason was waiting at the driveway curb for a carpool to take him to work. And then...in an instant...everything changed. Jason's younger brother, Michael, had been the last to see Jason hauling up trashcans. Shortly after that, Jason vanished and a family was brutally torn apart.

Can you even imagine?

Some skeptics might be mumbling that maybe the nineteen-year-old just ran away. Hardly.

Here was a kid devoted to his family who had read a passage from Romans in church the week before. He was dressed in his work clothes and dress shoes. He had a paycheck at work waiting for him. There was no activity in his bank account. His car was waiting to be picked up at the repair shop.

No, Jason did not run away. He was stolen.

He was stolen from his family. He was stolen from his friends. He was stolen from his life.

Having someone you know inexplicably disappear doesn't happen to everyone, but it is a far more frequent occurrence than we dare to believe. Each year, over 850,000 cases of disappearances are reported. Most cases find resolution eventually...but Jason's case is one of 105,000 cases in the United States for which there just hasn't been an answer.

Come with me for a second to consider what that experience must have been like for the Jolkowski family. Is there even a word in the English language that could describe the ultimate pain of Kelly and Jim...Jason's parents? Undoubtedly, it was an anguish and despair taken to the most extreme of levels. Pray to God that you and I never have to experience what that actually feels like.

Having a family member disappear without a trace is harder than anything I can imagine. If someone dies...even immediately... you know what happened. If someone leaves your house and never returns...at least there was a chance for a parting good-bye and a big hug. None of this happened in the Jolkowski story. There was no farewell hug...no "I'm okay" phone call...no letter of explanation.

There was nothing. Except endless grief and wondering:

"*Where did he go? What happened?*"

And even though years have passed, the pain remains the same. It never goes away. And there is nothing you can do about it.

Except maybe help others.

That's what Kelly Jolkowski is doing.

First, she helped others by bringing awareness of the Missing Person problem to center stage in the state of Nebraska. Nebraska had no true clearinghouse to provide and disseminate information about missing persons between local, state and federal agencies. On May 25, 2005, ***LB 11, Jason's Law***, passed...and that problem was resolved.

Second, Kelly continued her action mode and began helping other families across the country who were also coping with the brutal trauma of a loved one's disappearance. Kelly knew that for her to move forward, she had to help others move forward, too. Therefore, after *Jason's Law*, she created ***Project Jason***.

As of this writing, *Project Jason* has distributed more than 15,000 personal ID kits, facilitated the distribution of more than 50,000 posters nationwide, given out nearly 5,000 missing person photo buttons, and regularly disseminates information about new missing people in monthly trucker magazines. *Project Jason* has played a role in legislation being passed in six states that positively affects missing persons cases, which has made a direct difference in locating a number of missing people, including a teen missing for two years, a sister missing for seven years, and a son missing for fourteen years. Since its inception, *Project Jason* has helped over a thousand families cope with their real-life nightmare.

Can you imagine how hard it would be if someone you cared about disappeared? Can you imagine how easy it would be not to go to work…to become anti-social…to hate the world? Can you imagine how easy it would be to quit on life?

I can.

It is, however, inspiring to learn that there are amazingly strong people like Kelly Jolkowski in the world who have walked through the hottest of fires. People like Kelly give us strength to face our own battles. They put in perspective what really matters in life.

"*The small things never bother me anymore. Really…what's getting a flat tire compared to losing your son?*"

The next time you start complaining about bad luck…stop. The next time you mutter about how hard your life is…catch yourself. Because in comparison to what you may be experiencing, there are others who are living through far more intense storms.

And they are surviving.

It puts so much of our day-to-day stress into perspective… doesn't it?

PLANTING SEEDS

All across the country, my interviews were held indoors. Except for one special day.

I was in downtown Fort Wayne, Indiana, looking down from the stands at one of the most beautiful baseball parks I had ever seen. Modeled after Wrigley Field in Chicago, the home of the Tin Caps is a baseball fan's dream. Furthermore, any ballplayer with the opportunity to put on a glove and chase down fly balls in the outfield is pretty lucky. Parkview Field feels as close to the big time as one can get without stepping into a real major league stadium.

Looking down upon the field this beautiful September day, I thought: *To heck with the conference room! Let's interview people outside!*

And that's what we did.

We set up our Fort Wayne interview show right there on the plateau...above the stands...looking down on the dream field. The stage had been set for a unique day.

For the most part, my interviews with the *extra mile America people* I met started out as missions of inquiry:

"*So tell me about you...and what you do.*"

Although I always knew the basic background of each person beforehand, I found it helpful to hear their unique story from their own point-of-view before posing my questions. After this initial telling, conversation would flow and a rapport would usually be established. Eventually, answers started pointing to "*This is why I do this.*" That's where a true glimpse into the person's deeply planted passion would begin to show. That was the part that I loved. That's where my own *big picture* seeds were being watered.

While enjoying my day in Fort Wayne and meeting a whole cast of great people, I was told the story of a famous historical character who was buried nearby...Johnny Appleseed. As a kid, I remembered hearing...or reading...about this wilderness wandering man who planted apple seeds throughout the countryside.

The stories share that Johnny...with a bag of apple seeds hanging over his shoulder...would go walking into the wilderness, and when he found a good place to plant, he would clear the land by hand and then plant his seeds in nice, neat rows. Some of his planting areas were even over an acre in size. The "Apple Tree Man," as he was sometimes known, would then sell the growing trees to pioneer families so they, too, would be able to begin their own apple orchards and enjoy the beautifully blossoming trees around their cabins.

The unique story of a passionate man with a dream was all very fitting. It was a reminder that it's a good thing to honor our uniqueness. Often I have found myself watering down my own individuality in order to fit in and do what I was "supposed" to do in life. Looking at the "This Is What You Are Supposed To Do Rule Book" society encourages us to follow, leads us to care more about what others may think rather than what our individual hearts may feel. Having made that mistake, I have found myself terribly unfulfilled. When I have done that, it seems I temporarily lose a bit of my own identity...and the end result is that my own contribution to the world lessens significantly.

Neither is a good thing.

Sitting outside at the stadium that day listening to the stories of a number of people who were not watering down their uniqueness and contributions, I met a woman out of the Johnny Appleseed mold. And although ninety-year-old Airport Ambassador Mary Gebhard wasn't sharing apple seeds with others, she was sharing cookies with passengers coming in and out of Fort Wayne's airport. Like Johhny, Mary was living her passion, and in doing so, she was making the world a better place. Both Mary and Mr. Appleseed were unafraid to be themselves…to be unique.

Whether or not we are passing out cookies or dropping a few fruit seeds in the ground, we are all planters of one kind or another. Everywhere we go, we are each planting seeds. It could be in our words. It could be in our actions. The result of our seed-planting… good or bad…will always be felt and measured by the person we immediately touched.

It's good to remember our seed-planting roles.

It's also good to remember the seed that has been planted individually in each one of us.

Just as we each are individual in appearance, voice and personality, we also are unique in the purpose of our being. Deep inside the core of each of us is a seed of individuality and potential unique to who we are. It's the seed that makes us an individual. It's the seed that allows us the opportunity to make a difference in our world. It's the seed that contains our true voice.

Some of us may hand out cookies to strangers, plant beautiful apple orchards for future generations to enjoy, or ride a bike across the country encouraging others. Regardless, each of us are important to the whole, and I believe each person has the possibility of sparking a future chain of events that can make the world better.

As I look to the future, you can rest assured that I will honor the seed of potential that is planted in me. You can also count on me carrying my own version of Johnny Appleseed's seed bag over my shoulder, digging my hand into it often in order to grab a handful of seeds, and throwing them out into the world as I walk.

I hope you'll join me in planting.

EXTRA MILE HERO

Would You Put Giant Mouse Ears On Your Car?

...being dramatic to make a difference

I'll tell you, it's pretty hard to ignore Ruth Leacock and her mission. I mean, c'mon...really? Who believes in their cause enough to drive around town with GIANT mouse ears on top of a car?

Ruth Leacock does.

It's because this super energetic grandmother loves Africa that darn much. The mouse ears on the car? They're symbolic.

She and her co-creator (husband Tim) have been on a decade-long mission to send refurbished computers to Africa. The mouse ears on top of the car that she boldly drives around town is her way of saying that even a simple computer mouse can grow up and have big dreams.

Like going to Africa.

By the end of 2009, ***Computers For Africa*** had sent almost 1,900 computers to Uganda. Those computers have served 117 schools and benefited 60,000 students.

Impressive, huh?

The idea originated in 1999 when Tim and Ruth collected computers from friends and businesses and shipped them to Africa in a half-filled twenty-foot container. From there, the commitment kept growing. And when I say the commitment kept growing, I mean it really kept growing.

They even moved to Africa.

In 2004, the Leacocks put everything they owned in a ten by fourteen storage area and moved to Uganda for two years. Kids and grandkids were given one final big hug and left behind. They said good-bye to friends. They said good-bye to the United States.

When you are people with an *extra-mile* mission, sometimes you really just have to *go the extra mile*. Even if it means going to the other side of the globe.

After meeting Ruth Leacock, I had reason to stop and question the size of my own life vision and commitment. Would I do something as drastic for my mission as move to Africa? Would I be so bold and up-front about my commitment that I would do something similar to driving around with giant mouse ears on my car?

I'm questioning my answers.

Up to this point in my life, my personal vision had never extended much farther than the United States. Could I really dare think of speaking internationally? If I ever do, I know whom to thank for planting that seed. But please, Ruth, don't be offended if I skip the mouse ears.

Or wait...should I?

In total commitment, passion, vision, and creativity this *extra mile* grandma who drives around Omaha, Nebraska, has sparked my imagination as much as anybody I met on my journey of over four thousand miles. She is dramatic in the size of her dreams. She is even more dramatic in the actions it takes to achieve them.

Ruth reminds all of us that some goals require finding a little extra courage to climb up the additional rungs to the swimming pool high dive. Just jumping off the low board might not be enough to cause the sort of difference-making splash a bigger goal would create.

In a Ruth Leacock world, we can all dream of accomplishing goals bigger than ourselves...or goals even bigger than we ever thought possible.

After all, in Ruth's world, even a simple "mouse" dreams of accomplishing bigger things.

MEET JOE BROWN

We're surrounded by Joe Browns.

You might not think it, but all around you are some of the most intriguing and colorful characters…people…walking the earth. You don't have to watch television to see them either. They're right in front of you…living in your day-to-day world.

They work in the store where you buy groceries. They ride the elevator with you at work. You see them walk their dog by your house every evening at the same time. They whistle while they pump gas.

Yes…that's him or her. That's one of the world's very cool… colorful people.

The key to locating the colorful people?

1) Take your eyes off yourself.

2) Look around.

3) Don't be afraid to engage in conversation.

On the *Extra Mile America Tour*, although my eyes were wide open, I spent so much time by myself pedaling that when I did come across a new person, it was natural to want to engage in conversation and chat about most anything.

It's a good thing, or I would have missed out on meeting hundreds of interesting people.

Let's take just one day.

September 17th, Day 60 of the *Extra Mile America Tour*

I was riding from Columbus to Zanesville, Ohio. In pedaling distance, it was only 55 miles, but the ups-and-downs really begin to work you over…especially when you start out feeling tired. But being tired on a bike can have its benefits.

It makes you stop more. And when you stop, you meet people.

Brenda Sue. Joe Brown. Sue...the owner of ***Bud's Produce.***

Let me introduce you to each.

I met Brenda Sue first through a billboard along the road. It displayed her picture and an advertisement for the ***Central Ohio Opry***. A restaurant and singing joint...it featured, of course... Brenda Sue. I rode just a bit further, and there was the place.

"*Hmmm...this deserves a look!*" (You say that a lot when your legs are tired.)

Giving myself a much needed rest, I leaned my bike against a tree and walked across the street to the restaurant. It was lunchtime and although there were no customers, some good laughter definitely was going on inside. I recognized the first person who came into view from her prominently displayed picture on the marketing sign. It was Brenda Sue. Behind the non-alcoholic bar stood her niece. Her fiancé was also there.

"*So, you're the famous Brenda Sue, huh?*" I asked, already knowing.

We started sharing time, and I learned that she had always wanted to sing at the famous *Grand Ole Opry*...and since she never had that chance in life as yet,...she created the *Central Ohio Opry*. She had opened up this restaurant and bluegrass joint as a means of doing what she loved...singing and listening to good music.

Before I left, I just had to hear Brenda Sue sing. That wasn't hard. There was nothing insecure about ole Brenda Sue as all her pictures around the place signaled loudly. Before I knew it, her fiancé pulled out his guitar and she was sounding just like Patsy Cline from days gone by.

"*The old stuff is the best stuff,*" she told me.

Next down the road....a different Sue...from *Bud's Produce.*

Sue and her husband own a little produce store that sits on the corner of a very quiet country intersection. From the outside, it looked like an antique store, but upon closer inspection, I noticed a weathered "*Bud's Produce*" sign. I walked over and looked around, certain that I was going to find something unique.

In this very small and cramped store, the advertising signs were written by hand. Over an assortment of veggies one sign read: "*Grown local…like right down the street.*"

"*We're real local,*" Sue shared. "*If it isn't within a mile…it isn't local.*"

In talking to Sue about the history of *Bud's Produce*…and her own history…I learned that the store is open 360 days a year …always.

"*Closed Thanksgiving, December 24th and 25th, and January 1st and 2nd.*"

"*January 1st and 2nd?*" I asked.

"*Yes…I can't miss any of the college football bowl games!*"

And then there's a character I'll never forget…Joe Brown.

Joe was a crusty soul who converted an old barn into an antique shop. His store/barn was sitting out on a country road by itself, and when you passed Joe's faded-pink-with-paint-peeling store, you just had to go see what it was all about. I have to tell you, I have never seen more antiques piled into one area in my entire life. Joe is pretty darn good at collecting old things.

And he loves company.

We sat outside on his porch swing under the shade and talked. Mainly I listened, I suppose. His son had a big shrimp and fish farm up the road, and tomorrow was going to be a big shrimp-fishing day.

"*I take a buck and spend it. My son went to college...he takes a buck and makes another.*"

Joe wasn't only proud of his son's money making skills. He was also super proud of the Christmas sleighs he made. He pointed one out.

"*I sold three last year. They're pretty darn popular around here.*"

I was in Ohio and had learned that this state loved its football …and its football teams. Flying outside small homes in small towns everywhere was either a Browns' flag…or a Bengals' flag.

"*So Joe, who do you root for…Cleveland or Cincinnati?*" I asked.

Joe responded, "*I don't root for neither. In football, someone loses and someone wins. Someone's happy and someone's not. That's all football is…and I don't have time for that.*"

Before leaving I asked Julian to take a picture of me and ol' Joe.

"*That picture ain't going to go on America's Most Wanted…is it?*"

I wasn't sure if Joe was kidding or not, but for my own safety, I answered correctly.

Today had been a fun day with fun people…and great characters. With each, I had been given the chance to learn and to laugh; I had been given the chance to smile and connect. If I had met Brenda Sue, Joe Brown, or Sue from Bud's Produce back at home in California, I might not have ever had a chance to get to know them. I probably would have been too self-absorbed focusing on accomplishing every item on my "To Do" list.

And that would have been a shame.

Characters like these exist all around us. They're grown local… and not only on a country road thousands of miles away. We just have to take the time to get to know them.

The next time you have a chance to chat with a stranger…why not take the time, appreciate the opportunity and really chat. In the end, I guarantee an extra pinch of quality and flavor will be added to your day, and, undoubtedly, you will be the better for it.

Who knows? You might even get someone to sing to you.

Journal Entry September 17th:
The ride from Columbus to Zanesville, Ohio… the first day I noticed the leaves starting to change. I suppose, too, with the hills starting to increase in number…and my speed decreasing…I had more time to notice. The scenery is really striking in this part of the country. It feels so peaceful and every turn has so much character. I wish I had a camera on the front of my bike and could just keep clicking as I pedaled. Every turn…every hill…there is a new sight that makes you go "Wow!"

THE STING THAT WASN'T

I was pedaling into Cambridge, Ohio, when it happened.

STING!

Now the only thing in the world that gives me an allergic reaction is a bee sting, so naturally my brain went on red alert. My right hand immediately came down from my ear where I was holding a cell phone, and I slapped at what felt like an intense bee sting penetrating my thigh. Cast into total survival mode, my mind had communicated to my hand to abandon the cell phone.

And then...*STING TWO!*

I felt a similar sting on my left thigh!

Dual stings almost simultaneously were just too much to handle and my left hand squeezed the brakes super hard. Neither the right hand nor the left hand actions went as smoothly as my brain had intended. The end result was a cell phone flying fifteen feet in the air, and my body going air born over the handle bars.

Although it may seem like I made a regular practice of falling off the bike, please note this was never my intention. Furthermore, if I were to temporarily disregard memory of a few minor mishaps that caused me to be displaced from the bike seat, I really only had two bad spills on the trip. (Thank goodness for helmets and bike gloves!)

The reason for this bad fall, however, was unique. And it was extremely educational.

You see, this was the second time that the "bee sting" phenomenon had struck me. The first time had been just a couple of days prior when I was pedaling into Columbus, Ohio. Neither time had there really been a bee or any other thigh-attacking insect.

So besides the fact that both happened in Ohio, I knew there had to be an additional common thread. And there was.

As I contemplated more deeply the circumstances around both stinging events, I came to the bizarre conclusion that it was the electricity. Both "stings" occurred while I was riding under huge, buzzing power lines. (These are the power lines with the super thick, black, electrical cables that together conduct so much juice that I could hear the "*buzzzzz*" as I approached them.)

I had been shocked.

Doing a bit of Internet research that night at the hotel, I discovered a strange phenomenon where bicyclists riding metal bikes under these HUGE power lines experience electric shocks that feel like insect stings...and more often than not...the resulting shock was inside the legs of their bike shorts!

Hmmm...interesting.

The news was worth a definite chuckle.

Man...sometimes life gets a little crazy, doesn't it? Getting stung...without a bee...while riding a bike? Crazy stuff.

Occasionally, we feel the stings of life...imagined or not...and we get knocked to the ground. Sometimes we get hit with some out-of-the-blue news that really jolts us. But really...that's just life. It's going to happen. The stings will inevitably come, and the shocks might disable us for a short period. Then we rub the ouches and seek to find our stride one more time.

But the healthiest dose of medication I have ever found is when I just laugh at the craziness of it all. That keeps me going better than anything else I know.

Even with a bit of laughter, I can tell you...lesson learned. In the future, I will definitely have my eyes and ears peeled for those big buzzing lines. I can assure you, the next time I see those lines, I will walk my bike underneath them.

EXTRA MILE HERO

Climbing Mt. Ranier
...with two artificial eyes

It's not a thought we consider often, but we are far luckier than we think. It's easier to complain about our physiological make-up than to show gratitude in regard to the characteristics we are lucky to have.

"*I wish I were taller.*" "*I wish I had straight hair.*" "*I wish I had a different nose.*"

"*My ears are funny looking.*" "*My teeth are crooked.*" "*I hate my freckles.*" "*My eyes are too big.*"

Most of us have a list of our own "*I wish I could change...*" items. The items on this list are far more frequently acknowledged and muttered over by all of us rather than any single item on our "*Thank goodness I have...!*" list.

Just consider the following for a moment.

Most of us have two great legs to carry us from one spot to another. We have creative minds which allow us to think and problem-solve. We have taste buds that give us the opportunity to savor the sweetness of honey. We have a mouth and tongue which work perfectly fine in allowing us the ability to communicate.

We have ten toes that assist with walking and ten fingers that make picking things up and sticking a button through a slit so much easier. We have two ears with which to hear the singing of a bird outside our morning window. We have a nose that can inhale the fragrant smell of a mountain pine. We have two arms that can be wrapped around another human being. We have eyes with which to see the entire world around us.

In finding time to complain about our hair color and the lines around our eyes, we easily ignore some of the meaningful basics that a few people in society don't have.

Like Sheila Holzworth.

She has two glass eyes. She is totally blind.

Born in 1961, Sheila had her eyesight taken from her in a freak accident at the age of ten when the orthodontic headgear that was attached to her braces snapped and gouged her eyes. At that instant in time, Sheila's ability to see…one of the very basic characteristics we regularly take for granted…was taken from her.

Talk about a world changing in an instant, huh?

What would you do if you couldn't see to drive a car? What if you couldn't see the miracle touchdown catch that won the Super Bowl? What if you couldn't see a puppy's cute expression as he dragged his chew toy around the room? What if you couldn't see your child's first steps? What if you couldn't see how high the waves were?

What if you couldn't see the changing colors of fall or the brightness of the moon as you walked in the evening? What if you couldn't see the faces of those whom you love? What if you couldn't see the words in your favorite book or experience a movie on the big screen? Eliminating all of these special life moments would certainly cast doubt on the small inadequacies that are often the subject of our focus.

But for Sheila…she doesn't dwell on her lack of sight. In fact, she doesn't even let being blind stop her. At 48, she remains active… very, very active. In fact, in reviewing Sheila's accomplishments, you would never know she is blind.

Despite her blindness, Sheila has become an internationally known athlete whose accomplishments have included being the first blind woman to climb Mount Rainier, winning national and international competitions in downhill skiing, water skiing, and trick skiing. She has set world records. She has ridden a tandem bike across the state of Iowa. She has run marathons. She rides horses, jet skis, and snowmobiles.

And well, *holy cow!* What hasn't she done?

And again, do I need to remind you that she has two glass eyes?

I am inspired. Other guys named Reagan and Bush #1 were inspired, too, honoring Sheila at the White House on separate occasions.

Her life is definitely different from ours…isn't it?

Considering that she is completely blind, you, like me, may wonder how she accomplishes some of the things she does.

Shawn: "*How do you ride a snowmobile?*"

Sheila: "*With a communicator in my helmet so I can hear someone say, 'curve to your right…curve to your left.'*"

Shawn: "*How do you race down the ski slopes?*"

Sheila: "*I follow a person in front of me who shouts out, 'Turn!' 'Go faster!' I know that I am following the course if the snow from the person in front of me is hitting my chest.*

Amazing, huh? No fear. No excuses. Just all out.

"*I give credit to my parents. When I became blind, exceptions were not made for me. I still had to do dishes…I still had to clean dog kennels. Being blind was not an excuse.*"

I wouldn't even want to count how many excuses I have made for myself over the years because I thought I didn't have all the "goods." After having met Sheila Holzworth, all my excuses seem pretty darn inadequate.

If a person can climb one of the world's tallest mountains… blind… let's consider anew what you and I can climb in life...yes?

So if we allow ourselves an excuse to keep us from venturing boldly out...or we give in to complaining about a few wrinkles developing around our eyes...Sheila is a good person to remember.

She is also a good person to help us "see" that our insecurities and limitations exist only because we choose to allow them to exist.

ELI HERSENBERGER

It was on the side of the road near Old Washington, Ohio, where I met him. He was selling homemade baskets, walking canes, and an assortment of freshly baked pies on the corner just outside a gas station. The man was wearing a simple hat and a plain white shirt connected by a pair of suspenders to his worn trousers. Medium-built, he had a grey/white beard that had been left to grow free for years, but no mustache.

His name is Eli Hersenberger.

Oh yeah…and Eli is Amish.

At the time of our meeting, Eli was 61 years old, and, as I would come to learn, he had 19 kids...and 72 grandkids.

From the very beginning, everything about Eli interested me… from his horse and cart…to the excellent quality of his products… to his lifestyle choices. Being that the day was not too busy for either of us, I was given the privilege of asking lots of questions. Eli would smile back at me and give me lots of answers.

We chatted for thirty minutes.

We talked about a wide range of topics:

His beard—*never been shaved after turning eighteen.*

Amish dating habits—*they sit and talk.*

Traveling—*they can ride a bus when going long distances.*

Life regrets—"*It broke my heart when two boys left.*
But they came back…they usually do."

I had never had the privilege of sharing time one-on-one with someone Amish before, so the day was special. It was because there was something special about Eli, his beliefs, and the way he lived. I asked him about the 2006 school killing where a crazed outsider had come into a Pennsylvania Amish community and killed five young girls. What stood out in my mind was the unbelievable Amish response: *total forgiveness…zero anger.*

As Eli explained his faith to me, there was a calmness about him that seemed "other worldly." Perhaps I was so used to living on the "outside" that I thought anger, bitterness, and retribution were qualities that every human being would have felt. But no …not true.

Not the Amish.

Before I left, I bought a blackberry pie and asked if I could take a picture sitting in his horse cart. He obliged me, but kindly asked that he not be included in the photo. Sitting up on the cart, I felt a strange sense of peace and contentment. I imagined this to be a feeling that Eli experienced nearly every moment of every day. Just sitting there…after having shared time with this peaceful man… made me feel different. My friend Eli's purity and the simplicity with which he lived his life was transferred to me for a single moment in time. And it felt good.

As our time together came to a close, we each passed on our future blessings to the other.

Pedaling away on my bike, I pondered what it would be like to live like Eli. I almost wished I could. Something about his life just felt so comforting to my spirit.

It felt very, very good.

My brain rattled with self-questions:

Maybe I could live like that…couldn't I? Maybe I could live more simply and stress-free like Eli. Wouldn't that be awesome?

And then, I got on my cell phone to share my Eli experience.

GOD BLESS AMERICA!

One thing is certain: America has amazing diversity. Slowly riding a bike across the country makes that perfectly clear. From the inner city of Oakland, California, to the cornfields of McCook, Nebraska, America is as diverse in its people as it is in its geography. All of us seem to find our own place in the country…our own community where we feel comfortable and fit in.

One observation I made was that so many of the people I met who were born in small town America seemed to stay there. Now of course, I have no figures to support my little assumption…just some first-hand, on-the-ground detective work.

Question: "*So where are you from originally?*"

Answer: "*Born and raised right here.*"

I asked my question a hundred times and received practically the same answer the majority of those times.

It's easy to understand why, too. When you land in small town America, whether for a day or a lifetime, you are generously accepted. Most of the people are warm, helpful, and friendly. Quick to engage in conversation and eager to throw a supporting gesture your way, people in small towns are pure gold.

And they love their country.

In small towns, the American flag flies proudly in front of downtown stores…in front of homes…and in sticker-form on the bumpers of trucks old and new. Traveling through one town after the other, my own patriotism level increased two fold. Attitudes are contagious in small town America.

Nowhere was this more obvious than in Wheeling, West Virginia. I guess that's the sort of statement that can easily be made about a city nicknamed "*The Friendly City.*"

I had a late 7:00 P.M. interview with the Wheeling paper, *The Intelligencer*. The late interview was my good fortune because it gave Julian and I the chance to walk down to the river front and experience *The Sternwheel Festival*. Sitting ourselves down on the concrete steps with the locals, we were entertained by some old-fashioned, feel-good American entertainment. The spectacular fireworks show might have been the best I have ever seen…or should I say…"felt." Pure "*I love America*" music played simultaneously with the exploding colorful show…one great song after another. It just made my heart smile.

Afterwards, we enjoyed the concert tunes of a famous sixties group, The Marcels. Listening to a few classics including "High School Memories" and "Blue Moon" added to the evening's nostalgic touch. Being in Wheeling felt like walking back into American history. The whole night was perfect American nostalgia.

Except it wasn't "then."

It was "now."

Pedaling across the country, I experienced a sadness because towns like Wheeling are fading away from their glory days. Jobs are harder to locate and the locals are forced to head to bigger cities just to make a life.

It will be a sad day if the old-time American city eventually expires…but it seems inevitable. It's happening now.

I hope that big cities will one day be able to catch the heart-and-soul of *God Bless America* fever. I really hope that fever spreads with the population shift.

Until that day, watching fireworks in big cities just won't be as special.

EXTRA MILE HERO

Dreams For Kids

...sometimes even Santa needs a ride

When I met Tom Tuohy for the first time, he greeted me with a huge smile and a burst of energy. It was as sincere and powerful as if I'd just been reunited with a friend from the past. When Tom walks into a room, it becomes a special place not because he has arrived, but because he sees that YOU have.

"I love what you're doing! I love everything about the extra mile message! To quote Roger Staubach, 'There is no traffic jam on the extra mile!'"

You can tell Tom means what he says. Total passion radiates from every word and action that comes from him. It's the Tom Tuohy way.

But Tom isn't just a talker full of motivating energy.

He is also a big dreamer. And an even bigger doer.

Dreams for Kids...like many other great organizations' beginnings...had its roots planted in a simple act of giving. On December 24, 1989, Tom and a dozen volunteer friends visited a Chicago homeless shelter. At the shelter were 54 children whom, it seemed, Santa had forgotten.

But he really hadn't. Santa just needed Tom Tuohy to drive him there.

On that "miracle" night, Tom made a commitment to follow through every year with the same giving attitude and effort. It was on that night *Dreams for Kids* was born. Since that first miracle evening, 28,000 kids have benefited from the *Dreams for Kids* mission.

Today this organization has a presence in over thirty countries.

Great events and organizations are created from simple moments that move us. It is then that our hearts touch our minds…and our eyes are opened.

And we begin to dream.

Today, *Dreams for Kids* not only serves homeless and underprivileged children through its annual *Holiday for Hope* program, it also reaches out to kids who are developmentally and physically challenged with its *Extreme Recess* program. If a child is hurting…in any way…*Dreams for Kids* endeavors to ease the pain.

In a *Dreams for Kids* world, no child would ever be forgotten on Christmas, or be left wistfully looking at the playing field from the sideline. *Dreams for Kids* is all about giving disadvantaged kids the opportunity to live life just like any other kid, regardless of disabilities or limited finances. Children who are poor, homeless, or disabled...those are the children of *Dreams for Kids.*

Unfortunately as we get older, life sometimes grabs us by the shirt collar and tells us to quit dreaming and get serious about life. "*You're now an adult…and you have responsibilities!*"

As adults, we can choose to let the hideous "dream-killing monster" into our lives…or not. We are old enough to make the choice to believe or not believe its vitality-threatening words. But kids? They should never be allowed to meet such a balloon-popping fiend…regardless of the circumstances.

Sometimes someone has to step in and help manifest dreams for those who can't. *Dreams for Kids* does that. They create the opportunity. They pay the bills. And they even track Santa once a year to remind him of a few addresses that might have been left off his list.

On that initial Christmas Eve over twenty years ago, Tom Tuohy saw a need for a night. After that same Christmas Eve, Tom felt a need for a lifetime.

At any moment…on any day…our individual destinies…and as a result, the destinies of thousands of other people…can be changed in an instant. We first have to open up our hearts…then our eyes…and then care.

CONFLUENCE, PA

I'll never forget Confluence, Pennsylvania.

As I write this now, I am picturing this beautiful hidden town, tucked in a mountain valley along the *Great Allegheny Passage Bike Trail*. Confluence looks like an ideal setting in a Hollywood film. Everything is visually perfect.

Except Confluence, PA, has a very small quirk that might not be a big deal…unless you are without a car…very tired, very hungry, and need to make a phone call. Then, the perfect town shape-shifts from being a feel-good flick setting…into a drama, a comedy, and a thriller setting simultaneously.

On a bike, that's how I experienced Confluence, PA.

The particular day I rode into Confluence had been one of those hit-and-miss cell phone coverage days. Pedaling through the valley on a "*For Bikes Only*" trail, I was getting used to not having a regular phone signal. Having no phone coverage with which to touch bases with Julian was never too bad…unless, however, it started bordering on over two hours at a time without connecting. At a late point on this day, my legs were shot, and I hadn't talked to Julian in over four hours. The need for cell phone coverage was looming large.

I had shared with Julian at the beginning of the day to hold back on driving ahead until I called to tell him whether to meet me in the town of Confluence or Rockwood, where bike trail access was available to a car. The meeting spot depended on the state of my legs, and each town required him to take a different out-of-the-way route. Furthermore, it was hard to find the road a car could take to connect to a possible meet-up spot on the trail. It wasn't as easy as driving ahead and waiting for me in a town.

Arriving in Confluence, I needed some assistance. I needed rest, food and most urgently, I needed cell coverage. I began asking locals for guidance in where to catch a cell signal.

"*Every once in awhile if you stand in the middle of the bridge, you get a signal.*"

First, I tried that.

Every inch of the Confluence Bridge I explored…step-by-step… for a possible connecting signal. I shuffled forward…dialing…and listening for that connection tone. Each of the hundred times I tried…nothing.

Pedaling over to a couple of other folks to seek advice, I asked, "*Excuse me. Could you please tell me where I can get a cell signal?*"

The next three townspeople marked their ballot the exact same way: "*Three miles up the mountain.*"

As hard as I had tried to avoid the option of pedaling to the top of the mountain, it appeared my choices were down to only one. It had come to the inevitable. I was going up. It was apparent that this sucker was going to be a doozy, too. I could see some of the early bends and didn't need a super-sized protractor to tell me the angle up the hill was a sweet 45 degrees with twists and turns along the climb to the top.

If Confluence were to be a movie setting on this day…with me as the lead…the movie would be called *The Rockies…Part 2*. And for me to make this movie anything other than a weak drama with a poor ending, I would have to muster the strength of determination and will contained in every "*Rocky*" movie I had ever seen.

With no real food in my stomach for energy (one can only consume so many energy bars before the idea becomes nauseating), I lifted my leg over the bike like a 75-year-old man. And then I started pushing and climbing up the mountain…standing on my pedals…moving about as quickly as that same 75-year-old man would if he were beside me with his walker.

The mountain itself?

Let me tell you, my imagination had not deceived me; this was one steep dude. Regardless, I had a mission to climb the three miles to the top and find the spot where a friendly cell phone signal might find me. I did that whole positive self-talk thing...convincing myself over and over, *Just a little more...you're almost there....* The positive affirmation gig worked well climbing the *Colorado Rockies... Part 1*, and I was quite okay with hitting the rewind button again now.

Normally, an extra three miles out and back on a bike (six in total) is something you get used to on a cross country ride. It's easy to get lost crossing America, and I learned to live with the "small detour" and back-tracking possibility. Sure, you cuss a few times when it happens at first, but then you realize there is no choice but to go with the flow.

Changing the words pummeling your brain as fast as you can helps, too. I quickly learned that repeating *I'm an idiot!* just doesn't work for building much continued motivation.

Just a little more...you're almost there. Just a little more...you're almost there.

Finally reaching a church (*Yes! A church!*) on top of *Rocky Mountain 1.5* (my name for the Confluence mountain), I found my coverage. *Amen! Hallelujah!* Either word seemed the appropriate outburst now, and I was unafraid to mutter both through lungs that were gasping for air. It had been a very long and painful pedal...but in reaching the top, I wasted no time in pushing the numbers on the phone keypad one more time as fast as I could.

Success!

Eventually, after running all over town seeking out at least the faintest hint of a "*Can you hear me now?*" moment, I succeeded in getting my signal and setting up an afternoon rendezvous plan with Julian. Soon after that, I also found food and my body was re-energized.

Or wait...was I re-energized and then found food? I'm not sure which came first actually.

What was most important, though, was that at the end of my Confluence, PA, film-perfect day, there was a happy movie ending for an audience of at least one.

EXTRA MILE HERO

Fore Hope

...the magic of a little white ball

Her father really loved the game of golf. She really loved her dad. The two "loves" added together led this woman to the sport that would change her life...and thousands of other lives.

Perhaps at first, Mindy Derr's passion for golf stemmed from a desire to spend time with a father whom she saw as the greatest dad in the world. Or perhaps, it was just Dad's genetics kicking in making it impossible to avoid the destiny of the family's golfing DNA.

Either way, it became inevitable that this "daddy's girl" would find thrills in a game that chased a little white ball around acres of green grass.

At the beginning, golf was a bridge for Mindy. It was a bridge to fun and to enjoying nature. It was a bridge to challenge. It was a bridge to connecting with her dad as well as the other people she loved.

But in 1989, all those bridges came tumbling down.

Mindy's father...her golfing hero...lost his ability to speak and walk. Guy Derr became demobilized by one of life's most cruel and heart-breaking diseases...Lou Gehrig's disease. Gone was Guy Derr's fluid left-handed swing knocking the ball 250 yards down the fairway. Gone were his days of walking up the 18th green laughing beside his daughter.

Life had thrown a devastating blow to the Derr family.

It's uncomfortable to imagine stepping back in Derr family history in order to experience the broken-hearted pain. More than likely...in different ways...we each have been touched by a moment of devastation when our whole world collapses....when we feel life's super-hard and never-ending pinch on our heart. But Mindy's pain was not short lived. Watching someone slip away with Lou Gehrig's disease is a hard pinch that gets worse by the day. It's a disease that steals hope right in front of your eyes.

Mindy, however, was not about to let hope be stolen.

Utilizing every bridge-building lesson she had ever learned from the game of golf, Mindy Derr cast her vision on building her greatest golf bridge yet…a Columbus, Ohio-based therapy program called ***Fore Hope***.

With a desire to help her father get back on the course in any form possible, Mindy became aware that there were tens… hundreds…thousands…of people who were in her dad's shoes: people who had been sidelined from an active, participatory life because of a physical disability. Her father loving golf so much and not being able to play was unacceptable to Mindy. Call it "for the love of her father"…call it "for the love of the game…" but *Fore Hope* became Mindy's heart-felt passion, her overwhelming life purpose.

Mindy needed to find a way to get people who were disabled with crippling disease and disability like her dad back on the golf course where they felt most alive. She needed to find a way to help stroke victims down the fairway again. She wanted to help amputees hold onto and swing a club. Mindy knew golf's magical healing and rehabilitative powers could work miracles on those whose faith in miracles had been rattled, if only she could find a way.

What started as one person's challenge to help the disabled get back on the course has today turned into a national model for physical rehabilitation programs. What started out as a daughter's mission to support her father has turned into a giant lesson for the heart and mind. Mindy's lesson:

"If you really believe…talk yourself into it…and go for it!"

Over twenty years later, Mindy Derr's *Fore Hope* is stronger than ever. Through this program not only did Mindy find her life purpose…she has helped thousands of disabled golfers who weren't ready to have their last golf ball zipped into the bag.

And never once in the whole organizational-creating process did Mindy ever think small.

If you're going to think big and be associated with golf, why not hook up with the Professional Golf Association? She did. Why not hook up with one of golf's all-time greatest golfers? Again, she did. Today, her organization has a significant role in the Jack Nicklaus Memorial Golf Tournament.

Being a big thinker, Mindy also never short-changed the potential of her organization. She gave it everything she had.

She thought it important enough at the beginning of the whole chain of ideas to quit her job as an executive with the Boy Scouts of America. Sure, at that point in *Fore Hope*'s history, there was very little to hang her golf cap on…but she did it anyway. She left her financial security completely. Not only did she leave her paycheck behind by quitting her job, she invested every cent she had into building a viable organization capable of supporting the return of the handicapped to the golf course. In time, energy, money and personal sacrifice, Mindy gave the mission her all.

"My dad's illness taught me that once you get sick like this, you may never be able to participate in any activities again. I didn't want that. I had to give it everything."

Some people experience tragedy and fall into a life pattern of bitterness and defeat. Mindy Derr did the opposite. Mindy took her family's life tragedy and turned it into a miraculous blessing for others. She turned her father's illness and her own tears into a bridge that would help thousands smile once again.

Pretty cool response to tragedy, huh?

Now in my book, that's not only called "for the love of the game," it's also called "for the love of life."

And that's more than cool. That's inspiring.

HEALING

The strikes were adding up fast.

Strike 1: I woke up with massive fatigue, fluid in my chest, and strong flu-like symptoms.

Strike 2: It was raining very hard and the forecast reported: "*All day!*"

Strike 3: I missed the hotel breakfast.

Three strikes before 9:30 A.M. have been reasons in the past to take a mental-health day and just watch videos at home in "regroup mode." But today I couldn't. Time deadlines were so sensitive that I risked having to cut out a significant chunk of Tour miles if I didn't get on my bike and pedal. Regardless of how miserable I was feeling at that moment physically, I knew I would hurt mentally for the rest of my life if I skipped any miles.

I had to get out the hotel door.

Packing up my bags to be loaded in the van, though, I was struggling; I was really sick…the kind of sick that potentially knocks you down for a couple of weeks. I had only had that kind of illness a couple of times in my life, but this was a big reminder of times number one and two.

It's always been the norm for me that when I feel the "sick bugs" attacking my immune system, I jump into bed and sleep. I have learned to listen to my body when it isn't operating on all cylinders, and know that when I do, downtime turns from days into a few hours. Responding immediately by adding an extra round of sleep, instead of exerting more physical, mental, and emotional energy, I have always been able to heal quickly. My body is pretty darn good at playing the role of doctor if I just get out of my own way.

But today, I didn't have the luxury of adding extra sleep into my day. I had to ride. Sick or not. Rain or not.

This, however, created a big dilemma. I knew that it meant potentially taking a giant risk:

"*What if I got sicker?*"

At that moment, there seemed to be two distinct choices:

Choice #1: Don't ride.

Let my body heal, but accept the fact that I was not going to be able to complete all of the Tour's miles. Or...

Choice #2: Ride...and potentially risk getting sicker.

Both options were lousy, but the worst option of the two, to me, was #1...not covering all of the cross-country miles. I just had to do them all. I needed to.

At that moment, however, the possibility loomed large that if I didn't feel better soon—as in *immediately!*—I was in serious trouble. Honestly, this was the only time that doubt came rushing into my mind and that I ever thought to myself:

Uh oh...what if I don't get better? What if I can't finish this thing?

I wasn't sharing my feelings with anyone, but I was scared. It would be humiliating to me if I failed to make it across the country and had to stop. Regardless of the rain and how I was feeling, I plopped my butt on the bike.

Admittedly, one of the more insane things I did on this trip was waiting too long to buy adequate rain gear for riding, and because there was no place to make the purchase today, I would be riding in jeans.

Uh, huh...jeans. You can tell I am a true, big time professional rider, huh?

You have probably never had the experience of pedaling a bike wearing jeans for hours in the rain, but I have to tell you, it is one of the most uncomfortable feelings you can imagine. The jeans stuck to my skin like a glove one size to small. Every movement was a reminder of the discomfort. At first, I tried to rig homemade rain suit bottoms out of plastic garbage bags...punching my foot through the bottom of the bag. That worked for a few drier miles, until the pedaling motion of my legs tore the bags off completely.

Other parts of me were soaked, too. The towel I wore under my bike helmet to catch the water coming in through the air holes was drenched. My bike gloves were so wet that when I pushed on the handle bars… water oozed out of them. I was carrying what seemed like twenty extra pounds of water in my clothes.

And on top of that, it was very, very cold.

Wet, cold, and sick…I was barely holding on. Every ten miles I swallowed a couple of regular aspirins, hoping this might help kick the healing powers into high gear. However, what I believe really got me through that day…and on to that night's hotel room…was simply my own refusal to quit.

I was not going to stop myself.

You might question how much assistance can be found in healing affirmations. All day, I went to work on my thinking. I can tell you, I am a believer. Every breath…for hours that day…I was motivated to keep repeating the most simple of phrases: "*Breathe in health…breathe out sick.*" For miles and miles of muddy trail riding, I muttered this positive affirmation under my breath. Nothing else. Just that.

I was too afraid to stop repeating it:

"*Breathe in health…breathe out sick.*"

Now a medical doctor may proclaim that repeating the affirmation had little to do with helping me heal. But having lived through this day first hand, to anyone who doubts the power of positive affirmations, I would forever say: "*Believe!*" Beside the aspirin, this was the only medicine I used…and I truly believe it was the very best medicine I could have taken.

Our brains are mysterious. They are powerful. And when the magnificent mechanism we wear on our shoulders is used in the right way, the magical potential is unlimited. On this day…to me…it was all quite clear. I convinced myself that I was healthy.

For eight hours, I communicated the "*Breathe in health...breathe out sick,*" message to my brain and body.

And it got it.

I got it.

The facts were that at the beginning of the day I had a skyrocketing fever. I was flu-achy all over and had phlegm building in my chest. It was freezing outside, and the raining was pouring ...not sprinkling...all day. But I made it through sixty miles of bike riding. I made it back to a warm and dry hotel room where I could go to bed early and sleep uninterrupted for twelve hours.

And heal.

I believe that when we give ourselves the option to lose...it becomes an option. When we don't give ourselves this option... our brains and bodies take it out of the realm of possibility and do whatever they can to problem-solve...and produce the desired results.

"*Breathe in health...breathe out sick.*"

Repeated for hours.

I told my brain and body exactly what was happening...and it heard me. There was no way I could miss riding on that day. There was no way I could miss covering the crucial miles. And I missed neither.

The next day when I woke to ride again? It was still raining. It was still cold.

But I was no longer sick.

FRIENDS

It's good to have friends....not just people you call "friends," but the kind of people that you can count on when you're down-and-out. You know the ones I am referring to. They show up to applaud you in good times without jealousy and stand by your side during bad times without judgment. They're the ones who never elevate their own egos at your expense, and always do they want the very best for you.

I have been blessed by having some exceptional friends who at various times in my life have come through for me with shining colors. To my friends who have always been there for me? Thank you very, very much...you're the best!

I hope you have been as lucky.

Another great thing about having friends is that there is no rule regarding how many of them we can have. There are no limitations, and I would rather be the proud owner of one million friends than have a million dollars in my checking account. Personally, my life has been made much richer by the conversations and experiences I have shared rather than by the cars I have driven or what I have owned.

Maybe you'd agree.

On my ninety-day bike trip, I was lucky to add some new people to my "good friend" list. A number of people whom I interviewed, and a few great people I met on the road, have earned my friend loyalty forever.

One person in particular is my ideal of a true friend.

His name is *Dale Shultz.*

Dale is a Pennsylvania heavy equipment operator for a local coal mining company and is one of the most decent and honorable gentlemen you'd ever meet. Think any one of a number of Jimmy Stewart roles, add a little Lance Armstrong (the cyclist), a great big country heart, and there you have my new friend, Dale.

I met Dale during the last ten miles on one day's ride. My tail was dragging big time, and I was on one of Pennsylvania's bike trails standing in the middle of a bridge when Dale went zipping by me on his bike. At that exact moment, I was non-actively pursuing a two-goal mission: 1) resting with limited movement, and 2) enjoying the amazing beauty of the river. The sun was setting and the colors on both banks of the river were exploding because of the special late afternoon light. I had been on the bridge for about fifteen minutes soaking in the scenery and trying to memorize the picture for my mental scrapbook when Dale passed me.

I hesitated for about sixty seconds, then thought, *There's your rabbit! Follow that guy!* I needed an adrenaline kick to finish the day's ride, and Dale, minus the rabbit ears, looked like just the rabbit I needed. When you're super tired, the sun is setting, and you still have ten miles to pedal, you look for all the assistance you can find to pull you across the finish line.

Dale would be my push and pull.

After chasing him for a few miles—"*Who is that guy chasing me?*" he shared later—the man in jeans slowed down and let me pull alongside him. The conversation was warm and easy and he helped distract my tired body long enough to get to the day's finish line. Dale was a few months shy of his 55th birthday. He had just ridden from his home in Meyersdale, PA, 58 miles down the trail, and then turned around. That was down 58…and back 58. This is where Dale earns his Lance Armstrong likeness.

And Dale pedals fast.

Although we bonded greatly on that first day and first ride together…one of those great immediate connections…this is not where Dale earned his "*Friend Forever*" title.

The next day it was pouring buckets of rain all day, and the bike trail was super sloppy. I had already pedaled about fifteen miles or so when I stopped at the historic train depot right off the trail in Meyersdale. I was so dirty from the mud splashing off my tires that I looked like I had rolled in it. Finding the restroom, I used a hundred necessary paper towels to clean up and look normal again. When I stepped out of the restroom, two women working in the museum asked me, "*Hey...are you Dale's friend? Are you the guy from California riding your bike across the country?*"

Apparently, Dale had been my PR guy and had stopped by the museum earlier that morning and told them the story of our riding together on the previous day. He asked them if I had passed through yet. Now that they had encountered me, they got on the phone to call Dale.

"*Your guy's here, Dale!*"

Within ten minutes on a very messy day, Dale and his wife of thirty-five years, Rhonda, came down to see me. I was happy to see him again, and together, all of us did the picture thing. Dale and I chatted a bit more, and he showed me a huge zillion-year-old fern fossil now in the museum that he had uncovered with a drag line while digging coal in the mountain. It felt good to spend a few more minutes with him before I had to get back out and pedal in the rain on the slippery mud trail.

Dale helped Julian and I decide upon a meeting spot down the road in Frostburg, a place where we could find each other again. I got on my bike one more time with hopes of getting through the day's wet ride during one last big push. Seeing Dale had most certainly given me a small dose of encouragement to keep going. Having people clap for you always helps.

Maybe I can finish today, I thought to myself. My optimism... despite weather conditions...was brightening.

I made it to the next meet-up location very eager to jump in the van for permanent escape from the precipitation despite still being miles short of the day's original goal. *I'll make up these miles tomorrow,* I thought. *No way can I go any further in this weather!*

But there was a problem with my "*Get in the van now!*" plan. Julian and the van weren't there. I was standing out in the elements...

cold and dripping... with no van transportation. Phone calls were not going through (again!) indicating I was obviously in another no-cell zone.

"*Oh boy...what do I do?*" (That's not what I really said, but that's what I will paraphrase here.)

There was a sign indicating a town up the hill off the trail, and I started to push my bike up the steep hill. The rain had completely watered down my spirit, and I had no "pedal juice" left. I walked.

Suddenly...tearing down the hill toward me fast...two vehicles appeared from out of nowhere. The first vehicle I didn't recognize, but I could swear the second vehicle was my white support van. Both drivers pulled over upon seeing me. Out jumped Dale from vehicle #1 and Julian was in vehicle #2. I had been found!

Dale had helped Julian navigate the complicated set of roads to meet me. And knowing, too, what my total ride goal had been at the beginning of the day, Dale had gone home and loaded up his bike. He was ready to join me riding to the original goal...on one of the wettest days I have ever experienced...on a mud trail so slick that my tires were slipping constantly. I might have been partially crazy to be riding on a day like this...true...but here was a true friend about to jump in the deep end of the pool with me and pedal twenty more miles!

I did a quick and total dry clothes change in the back of the van with hopes of adding some temporary warmth to my icy flesh. Then Dale and I were off, riding together again. It seemed like an adventure that two third graders from yesteryear just couldn't pass up.

And we didn't.

Twenty miles on a bike have never gone by so fast...with tires splashing in the mud and water...Dale and I talked and laughed non-stop all the way to Cumberland. We were just two old...I mean "young"...guys out creating a great memory that will live with both of us for the rest of our lives.

Real friends? They don't let a downpour stop them from showing up for you. They don't care if they get muddy. They don't care if their hands turn bright red from the cold. They're just there…100%. They don't complain. They find a way to make you smile instead. They find a way to make a terrible day into one of your very best days ever.

A couple hours later, Rhonda and Julian tracked us down at the end of the trail in Cumberland. The day that had been so gloomy to contemplate at the beginning became one of the greatest adventures of my whole life.

And it was all because of a friend.

A really, really good friend.

Journal Entry September 17

I passed the Mason Dixon Line…and a big "Welcome to Maryland" sign. I was in a new state! I went through the longest tunnel of my life…Big Savage. This 1911 tunnel carved out through the center of the mountain was about 3/4 miles in length. The experience was surreal. The tunnel just seemed to keep going and going with flickering ceiling lights showing me the way forward. In spots where the lights were burned out, I rode in blackness guided only by the ceiling light 20+ yards up ahead. It felt like a scene from "The Twilight Zone"…and I was starring in it.

EXTRA MILE HERO

Helping Heroes

...a mom's commitment to do her part

It takes a lot of courage to join the military. For people who enlist, it's that very public acknowledgement: "*I love my country...and I am proud to be an American!*" For many enlistees, that potentially means going to a far away land and maybe not returning alive.

Good grief...that's heavy stuff! That's real pride. That's real commitment.

I remember back to that period in my life when it was announced that young men...or old boys...had to go down to the post office and fill out the paperwork declaring themselves eligible to be drafted. I really had no idea what it meant when I did it, but I remember my mom cried. The draft was never re-installed to my mother's deep joy, but many moms today feel what my mother felt over thirty years ago.

Multiplied by 100.

Their "person" is doing more than registering for the draft. He or she is joining.

First, I can't even imagine what it would be like to sign my name to all the forms required to give myself to a branch of the Armed Services. I suppose it's a moment during which a combination of great pride...and a ton of fear...melt into one. Chances are great that the signing of enlistment papers may be the one day that can re-direct the course of a person's life more than any other.

Heady stuff...again.

Thank goodness for all of America that there are brave and

committed individuals willing to sign their names on those enlistment forms. Amen, huh?

When an enlistee's signature does hit the dotted line, there is a whole bunch of other people affected, too. These are the moms, dads, brothers and sisters. These are the grandparents, aunts and uncles. These are the wives, husbands, sons and daughters. These are the neighbors, friends and co-workers. Many of these people may remain at home, but all are uniquely affected. Life may become more difficult. Every day, many are facing the challenges of the world without their "person" at home…and every day they are more than likely casting heartfelt prayers into the Universe.

"*Please bring my person home safely.*"

It must be hard: waiting, wondering, and wishing. These are not easy things to do, but they are each better than thinking about the biggest "w" of them all…war.

There is a group of family members and friends, however, who don't have it in their spirits simply to sit around and wait for their person to come home. Individually, they each feel a burning desire to do what they can to get involved; they need to do their part, too. These people are part of an extended military family not sent overseas but "enlisted" in a unique organization: ***Operation Homefront.***

Operation Homefront serves as a guiding force that assists in holding things together for a family while a soldier is away. The group provides emergency aid such as food, baby items, and help with vehicle repairs for families back home. They offer computer access, if needed, so a family can stay in touch with a loved one. If a soldier comes home wounded, *Operation Homefront* steps forward again to help the hero in every way possible. In all of these cases, members of the organization are eager to jump to the front of the "*I'll help you!*" line when a military family is struggling.

Operation Homefront takes the sting out of many families' real-life struggles because worrying about your "person" is one sting enough for a family to endure.

I had the good fortune of interviewing one of the amazing 4,500 national volunteers of *Operation Homefront*...Rebecca Drobnick. There are more than 30,000 folks from Ohio serving in our country's military. Rebecca's son, Caleb, is one of them. When Caleb enlisted in the Ohio Army National Guard, Rebecca got on the Internet to see what she could do to show support as a mom. She discovered the national *Operation Homefront* organization, but unfortunately, no chapter existed in Ohio.

Rebecca went to work starting one.

During her first Christmas as the new Chapter President, Rebecca threw her total energy into a toy drive. Many leaders lead by pointing a finger and telling someone else, "*Go do that!*" But not Rebecca. She led the toy project by driving her red Dodge truck all over the state...making a pit-stop at 167 Ohio stores...and personally picking up over a 140,000 toys.

I think that kind of individual effort is worthy of note in the record books.

In total, the whole toy drive project was a huge success with 282,000 toys collected. Kids belonging to military families in Ohio received fifteen to twenty toys each...and maybe for just a moment...they could apply their attention to something other than, "*When is Daddy coming home?*"

Two years after the initial event, this single mom has gone to work developing a strong statewide support team. She has found key leaders in the nine largest Ohio cities and has "enlisted" the support of over 300 volunteers to help the "*military family*" cause. Rebecca's role has been so inspiring, focused, and results-oriented, that the national organization has since lured Rebecca away from her full-time office manager job and created Ohio's first paid *Operation Homefront* position.

Do what you love with enough passion long enough, and people will notice you. That's what a mentor somewhere along life's teaching path has shared. Rebecca's real life success proves that it is true.

"I eat, sleep, and drink Operation Homefront. If my son can do his part in the National Guard, I can do my part to help the men and women like my son."

For many military families sending their person overseas, there is a sense of lingering hopelessness. Their person can't be protected by hugging arms or any walls of safety that can be constructed. A family's only solace is prayer. And supporting each other.

"So much of the time when I talk to another mom or wife, I just want to stand there and hold their hand and listen. As a mom, you are feeling their fear."

Ohio is the #4 state in the Union when it comes to military fatalities. It's just the ugly fact that comes with the "w" hardest to discuss. And until the greatest miracle in the world chooses to embrace mankind...world peace...there will continue to be families who receive their "person" with heartbroken tears when he or she returns home.

It's not right. It's not fair. It is terribly sad.

But thank goodness for people like Rebecca...and thousands of others like her...who care enough to hold hands and lead the charge in supplementing the financial and emotional support that is sometimes needed.

Until the day when the miracle of world peace is christened down upon mankind, it's great to have miracle people like Rebecca Drobnick in the world. And if your "person" ever becomes the "property of the US Government," my prayer for you is that you are surrounded by miracles just like her.

LAND OF THE LOST

You're out in the boonies. And when I say boonies…I mean no people, no cars, no cell coverage…but lots of wild things all around you.

Oh, and let me emphasize…you are alone.

Depending on the time of day and the distance between "boonies" and "non-boonies," you could have a problem on your hands that begins to wreak emotional havoc over your nervous system.

On one particular afternoon after leaving not-so-big Morris, Illinois, I found myself in the boonies. Now for the most part, I had grown accustomed to being out in the middle of nowhere by myself riding a bike along uninhabited dirt trails. But today the trail seemed truly removed from civilization. During one stretch of the day, I had not seen Julian or heard from him for over ten hours.

The separation from Julian started when I hit rendezvous spot #1 in Oldtown. No Julian. It continued at meet-up spot #2: Paw Paw. Again, Julian was MIA. Still, it was only 3:45 in the afternoon and I had made decent time getting to this next point. But I had no idea if Julian had come and gone…or where he was.

When one guy is pedaling a bike on an unknown dirt road, and one guy is driving in a van, it's tough to calculate a meet-up time. For me, meeting twenty-five miles down the road could take one hour. It could take four hours. It just all depends. If we missed one meet-up spot, it threw the next meet-up spot all out of whack because Julian never knew if I was in front of him or behind him.

We now had missed two meet-up spots and there was no cell service or way to communicate. What to do?

I couldn't be sure if Julian thought he had missed me and gone ahead…if he was still at spot #1…or if he had gone ahead even further to spot #3. There had been NO final destination set on this particular day. It was one of those "*I'm going to keep going for as long and far as I can*" days.

When you don't have a solid plan, things can really fall apart.

Fast.

I am about ten times better moving forward in life versus holding back, so my decision was absolutely predictable.

At 4:10, after hanging around for the eternity of 25 minutes at meet-up spot #2, I jumped back on my two wheels and decided to knock the next 17 miles off my mileage chart.

Bad call.

After I reached a few miles down the path, I noticed the trees were getting thicker and the canopy forming over me was blocking daylight. The sun was already fading in the day more quickly, but with trees also blocking the sun it was getting dark….really, really dark.

And cold.

Constantly, I would keep checking to see if I could get a cell phone signal. After hours of trying…and nothing…I finally did, but my call went straight to Julian's voice mail. I had a connection. He didn't.

Not to take a chance with losing my window of cell opportunity, I called Sacramento to relay a message of what was happening. Christine might have been a couple thousand miles away, but I needed her help. "*Get a hold of Julian! Tell him I'm heading to Little Orleans!*"

I finally made the 17 miles required to a get to Little Orleans…a town so small there was almost nothing there. Including Julian. It was time to get scared now. It was 8:30 at night. It was freezing. I had no money.

But even worse…what had happened to Julian? Was he okay? Had he crashed in a ravine? Had he been hijacked? You know all the questions that invade your thoughts when you don't hear from somebody; I was asking each one of them.

With no battery left in my phone, I went into the only joint in the whole town…a small restaurant that was currently occupied by the owner, the 75-year-old waitress and two locals. They were each humored by my story and weren't quite sure if I was even telling the truth about having started my bike trip at the Pacific Ocean. I sensed that they thought I was a junior nut case coming up with a grand story.

One of the two locals let me use his phone, which was capable of mustering a cell signal, and I called home for help to figure out what to do. Since Christine had also not been able to reach Julian all day, it was decided that she would call the Cumberland Police Department, report the situation, and get some help to see if anything happened to Julian. At the same time, we would get police assistance in helping me back to Cumberland where I could find a place to stay for the night and also be able to have money wired to me.

Oh, brother…this was getting messy.

Before the plan went into full effect—before making the final plea for help—I asked Christine to wait thirty more minutes for a miracle. Then…finally…the miracle I had been hoping for came. The man at the bar's cell phone rang. It was for me.

Julian had called Christine from a pay phone he found in a town somewhere. He asked her if she had heard from me. She relayed, "*Little Orleans!*" and forty-five minutes later…at a very late hour of the night…I was reconnected with my driver, warm clothes…and the rest of my life.

Finally feeling relaxed enough to take a deep breath, I enjoyed a bowl of Maryland crab soup before we departed Little Orleans. Julian was safe. I was safe. The *Extra Mile America Tour* was safe. The world as I currently knew it was finally on track again.

Sometimes in life, action without a solid plan is useless. Everybody may be going gangbusters straight ahead…but with no destination in mind…everything can get squirrely.

Today had been a squirrely day. But it was a good day to learn a lesson to be remembered forever.

Always, always, always…put action on hold…until you have a plan.

Journal Entry September 27

I went through the darkest mountain tunnel yet—over half a mile—at Paw Paw. A water canal was below and to my left and it dropped what seemed like about eight feet from the path. The tunnel was so dark I couldn't even see the canal most of the time, but I knew the threatening water was always there waiting to catch me if I moved too far to the left.

The path I was walking was barely wide enough for me and my bike together. I kept scraping the tunnel wall on the right with my shoulder as I walked. I just focused on the very small pin-point of light at the open end of the tunnel in the distance. It seemed I was moving so slowly, and my brain started to play tricks on me.

Walking for over ten minutes in deep pitch black is no fun at all. And it's scary.

EXTRA MILE HERO

I Don't Have Good News

...getting through cancer one more time

Initially, I interviewed Dotti Bechtol in Pittsburgh because of the great work her organization, ***Health Hope Network***, had been doing for years and years. First started by a nurses' association dating back to the Civil War, this revitalized health support organization had found a big-time critical health care cause...helping stroke survivors.

Today, the organization could not have a more passionate Executive Director.

But as my time with Dotti continued, I got to know more about her not as a professional leader of an organization...but as a human being. It started with one of her answers:

"*I feel so much empathy when people's health goes down.*"

"*Why is that, Dotti? What gives you so much empathy? What have you experienced in your life related to health?*" (It's my experience that those who have "felt" things in the past can more easily relate to those who are "feeling" things in the present.)

And this is where the telling of Dotti's story really begins.

First, Dotti Bechtol is deeply sensitive to the plight of stroke victims and their families. Her grandfather had a stroke. Her father had three of them. She has felt the pain as a frontline witness and caretaker.

But looking through the window at another person's health hardship is still only the tip of where her "health empathy" begins. Dotti's even deeper personal connection with others experiencing real life health issues goes straight to the person whom she looks at every day in the mirror...herself. She has lived through her own potentially catastrophic health scares.

Dotti Bechtol is a breast cancer survivor. Twice.

In 2007 and 2008…using two different detection models… breast cancer cells were found. On two different occasions, Dotti had her doctor look her in the face and say, "*I don't have good news.*"

Yikes!

Having heard the "*You have cancer*" news twice, it's easy to see why Dotti has developed a super-sized empathy for others in all things health-related.

"*Neither time did I feel a lump. The first time, I was looking at the screen of a Breast Specific Gamma Imaging machine and I said, 'What's that spot?' The person doing the test said, 'That's a problem.'*"

"*Denial was my first response. 'I'll have to deal with this later…I have a meeting to attend.' The doctor made it clear that the meeting needed to be cancelled.*"

Soon after sitting down and really listening to the seriousness of what was happening in her body, Dotti began a radiation routine five days a week…thirty minutes a day…for seven, long weeks. Along with her radiation treatment came the lowest energy levels of her life.

And massive fear.

"*Of course, when you get the news you have cancer and go through the treatments… it's absolutely terrifying. At first, it took my confidence away that I was going to live a long life. Cancer throws you for a loop. It's easy to feel out of control.*

"*Although I felt my body had let me down, I knew I had to rally. I knew that if I turned my horrible news into a project, I could deal with that. I had handled challenges all of my life and succeeded. I am a 'control' person and I was determined to show this cancer who was in control.*"

Dotti's first diagnosis of cancer had been a total shock. There was no family history. She has long been a five-day-a-week gym enthusiast doing cross training, boxing, kick boxing, pilates, spin… you name it. She is an avid reader about heath and diet, and she makes sure to put good stuff…good energy…into her body.

But still, "*it*" happened.

Even with a fearless attitude, a super-charged healthy lifestyle, and no genetic inclination…the way she lived her life could not change Dotti's fate in having to address and live through cancer. And remember again…for Dotti…this wasn't just once. It was twice.

Cancer was detected the second time the following year. Dotti was just beginning to get her confidence mojo back when, "*Wham!*" …it happened again. This time, a mammogram found a tumor in her other breast.

Once again…the shudder.

Once again…the fear.

Once again…the questioning.

Once again…the treatment.

It takes a strong person to fight cancer once. It takes a mega-strong person to fight it again. That's Dotti Bechtol.

I wish you could meet Dotti. Your life would be the better for it. She lives with an all-out gusto and is great fun to be around. She lives with a contagious energy and passion. No matter what mood you may be in beforehand, it's easy to smile when you are with her. Her attitude…her smile…her vitality…she's just one of those high quality people who radiate life. Sometimes we meet people whose positive personality affects us strongly and we think, "*Wow! Who is this person?*"

To me, Dotti is one of those people.

She returned to college at 39 and graduated *Summa Cum Laude* at 43. Having worked her way up the ladder, Dottie was already a successful executive in the steel industry. But she wanted to prove that she could earn the diploma held by her peers in the industry. And if going back to college later in life, working a full-time job, and being a mother didn't have enough challenges…she chose to double major in Psychology and Economics.

Phew!

Oh…and by the way…Dotti Bechtol loves speed. Uh, huh… and she likes cars a lot. In fact, she races vintage cars that go

140 mph. In a typical race, there may be 160 drivers…four of them women…and one of them is 56-year-old Dotti Bechtol.

"Racing helps me relax. It helps me wash away the stress. When I am in the car…my mind focuses on nothing else. When I get out of my car after a race, I just feel a super exhausted, wonderful relaxation."

Today, Dotti leads a vibrant non-profit organization. Today, she goes to the gym and kick-boxes. Today she takes a chemo pill. Today, she races in a car at 140 mph. Today, Dotti Bechtol is living life the way she wants.

Dotti accepts her bad-luck-card draw and focuses on playing the hand the Universe has dealt her as best she can. She doesn't let age stop her. She doesn't let gender stop her. She doesn't let cancer stop her.

We can't control everything that happens to us. Life happens, and there will be surprises. But Dotti Bechtol does reminds us:

"We can control how we deal with the events that touch our world."

And often, it is how we deal with those events and circumstances that give us the sort of control that gets us out of the back seat of our own life and once again behind the steering wheel.

Education barriers? Age barriers? Health barriers? Gender barriers? They only matter if we let them matter. That's what Dotti…the race car driver from Pittsburgh… teaches me.

And you know what?

There may not be any other lesson I have ever learned that is so potentially life-changing.

QUIT BEING AFRAID!

Count me as one of the millions who have never had a fondness for snakes. All of those crawly things creep me out actually...the insects, the spiders...all of them.

I think it came from my days in Webloes. (That's where ten and eleven-year-olds go right after being a Cub Scout.) I remember a meeting one night to which a guy came with lots of snakes in all sorts of individually bound burlap bags. Some of the bags would wiggle on the ground...and from others came noises as they sat there waiting to be opened.

It wasn't something I was attracted to even back then.

I held the snakes, like the other boys...but the mystery snakes in the bags...the ones we were told were poisonous...they scared the devil out of me. Ever since then, I have been stuck on scared when it comes to looking at all creatures snake-like. Imagination, you know.

On the *Extra Mile America Tour,* however, I addressed my fear. It's uncertain if I am cured of my snake paranoia, but—I'll tell you what—I had a heck of an adrenaline rush...and a positive experience.

I was riding down one of those long, dirt roads in the middle of nowhere, and I had been on this road for a number of days. When you see no one else on the trail for over forty-eight hours, you start to get stir crazy wanting to talk with someone other than yourself. At the very least, you invite any experience that is different, just to wake up from your developing complacency.

I was about to have that experience.

Along this particular road, there were very few bicyclists so late in the fall. It was getting cold. The changing weather and winds had knocked leaves and branches down everywhere. In parts the road was deeply rutted because of storm erosion. Even for riders of mountain bikes, it was tough pedaling. Leaves often covered giant branches or tree roots that could easily upend a bike and its rider. I had to constantly watch where I was going.

Late in the day, I saw a black, thick branch ahead of me that stretched from one side of the ten-foot road to the other. As I closed in, however, it was apparent that this was not a branch but a giant, dark, black snake. Being near a river and in the middle of jungle-thick trees, I had no idea what type of snake this was or if it preferred water or trees, or what. I only knew it was big and black.

I know that's not a real snake classification, but to me…it fit perfectly.

Immediately upon classifying my fellow traveler, I jumped off my bike and started inching…and I mean inching…closer to get a better look. Man…this guy was thick! My mind quickly did that racing thing, wondering what it took to feed it. I didn't like that thought and began to retreat by inching backwards.

Frozen now, I stood watching the latter half of this enormous dude as it started to depart the path. Then I had an urge:

Quit being afraid! Touch him! Go now!

I don't know what in the world got a hold of me, but I set my bike to the ground and headed for the back end of this guy, the thing I feared. I was positive it couldn't see me so my courage…or my craziness…shouldn't get too much praise or attention. I let my hand slide over the back of his skin. Shiny, slippery, big…there was my fear sliding right through my fingertips.

My heart was pounding and I felt shear exhilaration. I had dared to encounter something I really, really disliked and distrusted. And I survived!

Upon my touch, the snake sped its movement across the path. It sensed something. Quickly, I darted a few feet farther up the road to peak behind the tree towards which it was heading. And there it was. Not the body, but the head was looking dead at me and appeared to be wondering: "*What's up, dude?*"

Or…was it thinking "*Payback*"? Or worse…was it thinking "*Dinner*"?

I darted back the eight yards to my bike and, seeing that the snake had completely left the road, I sped through, keeping my eyes wide open and focused on the road in case snake #1 called a cousin down the trail to tell him I was coming.

The remaining sixty minutes of the ride were great fun. I felt that awesome rush we can get when we step entirely out of our individual comfort zone. Sometimes it's touching a snake of which we are afraid; sometimes it's wading into the ocean we fear to swim; it may be leaving a job we have hated for years; it could be moving on from a bad relationship…whatever the one-time or lifetime fear is…stepping out of our comfort zone can be revitalizing.

And sometimes, too, stepping out of one comfort zone can give us the courage…and momentum…to step out of a few of the other comfort zones which may have been blocking our ultimate success and happiness.

And that is definitely a positive step.

Journal Entry September 25

On the trail today, I passed a sign that indicated General George Washington had come down the river...in a canoe... with his men...in this very same location. Excerpts from his diary were printed on the marker. It is very cool to imagine that 200+ years ago, the first President...before he became President... was out here in the boonies exploring...where I am exploring now.

EXTRA MILE HERO

One Delivery Truck
...100,000 happy families

After the initial "*This is what we do...*" introduction, the next part of the conversation went something like this:

Me: "*With only six staff members, you provided food for 100,000 different families last year...really?*" asked in questioning awe.
Her: "*Yes. We have 2,000 volunteers,*" answered in a matter-of-fact tone.
Me: "*You're also telling me that your organization distributes food to over 550 food kitchens...in five different states...every month...with ONE truck?*" asked in awe.
Her: "*Yes,*" answered again in a matter-of-fact tone.

I sat there looking at her...and she back at me. I was contemplating the scope and logistics of such an undertaking.
"*That's awesome!*" The words finally came out of my mouth.

I had never heard of the ***SHARE Food Program***, and as I sat there considering the logistics of ordering, storing, and delivering food to over five states, I was blown away. The logistics of coordinating my own "little" bike ride across the country had challenged me. So, this program had earned a Ph.D in "*Phenomenal Coordination*" in my mind.
As the leader of this masterpiece in *extra mile success*, Executive Director Steveanna Wynn seemed pretty nonchalant about the whole thing: "*For us, it's the routine. We're used to the hustle.*"
To the delight of east coast food kitchens responsible for feeding the homeless and poor...thank goodness this is all just "routine" for

SHARE. To Steveanna, the vibrant and entirely humble leader of this awesome food program, their efforts and story seemed to be no big deal.

But it is a big deal. Without *SHARE,* thousands and thousands of people would go hungry.

The *SHARE Food Program* accomplishes their massive goal of reaching out to 100,000 families in two ways:

1. ***SHARE* serves as the ultimate "neighborhood mom" feeding the "neighbor kids."**

SHARE earns this "mom" title because they take care of providing food to 550 food distribution centers a week. And...as the process unfolds...these "kids" (the churches, schools, shelters, and community centers) then reach out with their dinner bell to the poor and homeless in their respective communities:

"*Come...and we'll serve you a hot meal.*"

It all starts with what goes on in the 1,700 square foot cooler space, the 3,000 square foot freezer, and the 70,000 square foot enormous warehouse that serves as the largest food pantry imaginable. Once the cooler, freezer, and pantry are stocked from local food vendors, the *SHARE* delivery truck starts rolling. Yes...THE truck.

There is only one.

Despite there being only one truck, if there is a food shelter anywhere close to Pennsylvania, Delaware, Metro New York, New Jersey or the Maryland Eastern Shore, chances are pretty good that its food came from *SHARE.*

2. ***SHARE* also understands that families other than the homeless need help with their food bills.**

Individual families are able to purchase affordable, wholesome food packages for more than 50% below what normal stores would charge for the same combined products. But there is a catch to participation in this low cost, high quality food program. For each package of food purchased, *SHARE* asks that TWO hours of good-deed time be SHARED back with the community.

You need to volunteer. Somewhere.

You see, the *SHARE Food Program* has a creative "*Pass it Forward*" mentality. This isn't just a program about serving food; it's a program dedicated to helping people reconnect with their communities. With *SHARE*, food is not the only thing that should be shared freely, but also time helping your community.

Under the *SHARE* plan, everybody wins. Families get a big break on their food bills, and the community gets a big lift by volunteers donating hours. The *SHARE* motto:

"***Do good. Feel good. Eat good.***"

What does it take to make this all happen?

How about only six paid staff. That's it! Thank goodness, though, for the volunteer mentality *SHARE* sows because over two thousand volunteers also step forward each month to make this possible.

Only six paid staff...a huge pantry...one truck...2,000 volunteers... that's what it takes to significantly impact 100,000 families.

Man, you gotta' love people who dream big...don't you?

Dreamers like Steveanna Wynn and the *SHARE* team challenge us. They remind us how big an organization can grow with quality... and daily consistency. They further remind us that big success is all about people...serving them...and enlisting their support.

It is definitely true that with only a few committed people by your side, you truly can "feed" the masses.

"WAY TO GO!"

Do you know the very first state in the Union? I do now.

It's Delaware.

Living on the west coast, my knowledge about the state of Delaware was close to non-existent. I knew that Vice President Joe Biden came from Delaware and that it was geographically super small and one of the least populated states.

But here's two more truths about Delaware that might be news to you as well:

1. This state hidden close to the Atlantic Ocean ranks near the very top of the list in friendliness, kindness, and supportiveness, and...
2. The people of Delaware take *going the extra mile* seriously.

I learned all of this firsthand.

Into every city I ventured, fantastic support and assistance was offered to me from the local people and organizations on site. But nothing compared to what I experienced in the city "*IN the middle of it all*" ...WilmINgton, Delaware.

On my interview day in Delaware, I was taken care of by one of the most *extra mile* people I have ever met in my life...Clare Garrison. Clare planned every item of my Delaware day from morning to evening. She did it with precise excellence and organization, and she threw in a few surprises for fun.

There was an awards event where I was given the "Key to the City." There was an event in which I had the chance to share time with the gracious First Lady of the State, Carla Markell. I met the charismatic Secretary of Health and Social Services, Rita Landgraf and Mayor James Baker along with his very polished Chief of

Staff, Bill Montgomery. Wow! It seemed like I met a hundred great people.

And together, all of these people represented the most kind and down-to-earth group of leaders I have ever met.

They were real people. They didn't care to hang their hats on job titles or walk into a room with that "*Here I am!*" attitude. There was nothing pretentious about any one of them. They spoke with humility. They walked with an eye constantly on service to others. They recognized contribution and applauded it.

On the evening of my event day, I had the pleasure of sitting in the audience as Wilmington recognized some local heroes who had been providing outstanding service to the city from the shadows. Everybody in the filled-up City Council chambers cared…and listened…and shouted, "*Way to go!*"

To see, hear, and be a part of that felt really, really good.

Too often in life, we forget to clap for each other. Too often, we think the whole world revolves around us as individuals. The people in Delaware taught me that a self-centered attitude is not necessarily the norm everywhere. There are some places where others do come first.

I like that.

I may not know a whole bunch about the politics of the state, but I do know a whole bunch about the people. And, having a Vice President from a state like Delaware, I feel pretty sure we're represented by a down-to-earth guy who cares about us.

Because that's just the Delaware way.

After becoming the first state in the Union, I guess they've had a bit of time to get that part right. I mean, c'mon…you gotta' know there is something pretty special about any state that makes the Lady Bug its state insect.

EXTRA MILE HERO

I Wish I Woulda'

...facing the biggest questions of them all

When I think of Roxanne Black, it's impossible not to be greatly inspired. There are a several reasons why.

1. Roxanne is a total survivor. She is the epitome of shear toughness and has endured challenges that you and I will, hopefully, never know. She has lived through two kidney transplants and faced many moments where the truth of life's shortness has shouted in her ear. Not only has she made it victoriously through each of these moments, she moved forward boldly...personally and professionally.

2. Roxanne has a depth of spirit and quality that is extra-ordinary. After sharing ninety minutes in conversation with Roxanne, I walked away realizing that I had just met one of the most empowered people I have ever had the privilege of knowing. She thinks deeply...she feels deeply... and she makes every one of her days on earth count by sharing a message of inspiration and hope. With numerous "close call" days in her life...and having had her life touched by so many who have had their last day...Roxanne doesn't take life for granted.

3. Roxanne is a builder. She created ***Friends' Health Connection***, an organization built from the heart. Roxanne doesn't just "match up" people for love or business...she connects people who are in a life-threatening situation. They are physically sick...some very. In being a special matchmaker, Roxanne provides individuals with a

friend...a kindred spirit…who can relate to what they are individually experiencing. Roxanne has facilitated thousands upon thousands of relationships for people who needed support at... perhaps...the worst time in their lives.

A few more facts about Roxanne Black:

1. At age 15, Roxanne was diagnosed with Lupus, a disease that compromises the immune system. The result of this disease is serious kidney failure.

2. Roxanne has had two kidney transplants...the first at age 23. Her sister gave her a kidney in one of those amazing "*I love you so much!*" gestures. At age 30, unfortunately, Roxanne's donated kidney failed, and she went through the donation-search process again. This time her "life gift" came from an eight-month-old child whose life sadly was over. Roxanne's gone through it all: the surgeries, the chemo, the medicines, the scares, and the negative prognoses.

Most of us struggle through the "little" worries in life:

"*Will I ever find a job I love?*" ... "*Will the right person ever show up?*" ... "*How am I going to pay for that?*"

Roxanne created an organization that focuses on helping sick and dying people through questions ever bigger:

"*Am I going to live?*" ... "*Am I going to be alone in going through this process?*"

The big questions regarding life and death—few of us like to talk about them. But we'll all eventually face them.

That's inevitable.

Actually, it seems to me that the sooner we personally start to contemplate the shortness of our duration on earth…like Roxanne found herself forced to do…the more we will begin to develop quality in our lives. In most cases, when we start to live as if we don't have forever, how we spend our time and who we spend our time with undoubtedly changes.

Maybe you or I wouldn't create an amazing organization like *Friends' Health Connection*, but maybe we would start trying to bring smiles to a lot more people.

So, what would you do if you only had one month to live?

I'm pretty sure if we each take the time to sincerely think about this question, then use our answers to mold the way in which we live our remaining days, our "*I wish I woulda'...*" list will be much shorter when the time finally does come to say our last goodbyes.

ONE-EYED RIDING

Have you ever had a moment where you did the very thing you know you shouldn't have done? Let me tell you, I have had my share of those moments in life.

Don't do that, Shawn! I'm warning you...it won't turn out well!

That's kinda' how my internal voice plays in my head at times. Sometimes I listen. Sometimes I answer back:

Blah, blah, blah...be quiet!

The particular incident I'm about to share was one of those moments in which I should have listened...to myself. I should have slowed down a moment to think things through.

I was a couple of days outside of Washington, DC, coming into the city on a back-trail road. It was windy, big time. Branches were falling, leaves were swirling, and I could feel every small particle in the vicinity come swooping straight into my face.

And eyes.

For anybody who wears contact lenses, you know windy days are not good. The smallest grain or dirt particle that lands in your eye can really hurt. That's what was happening. I had a couple of small sand particles find residence in my eye and the normal blinking and eye-watering thing just wasn't working.

One particular particle of dirt...actually, it felt like an army of dirt particles...was setting up camp in my left eye. *Owww!* It had to be dealt with.

Being alone out in the middle of nowhere, I had no saline, no sink, no mirror...no nothing. Since I was about fifteen miles from the nearest *potential* eye-cleansing spot, I had to do contact lens emergency surgery right there on the road. My cleansing equipment, unfortunately, consisted of nothing more than an unsanitized pointing finger to remove the contact and a mouth for cleaning it off. I know it is not a pretty picture…but a guy has to do what a guy has to do.

Step #1 of my no-look contact removal was completed flawlessly. Contact extracted. (*Ahh!…*my eye felt better already!)

Step #2 was also completed without complication. Contact inserted into mouth for quick swishing and cleansing completed successfully.

Step #3…*uh oh!* While putting the contact back into my eye, a small gust of wind hit the tiny, hard-to-see object floating on my finger. The wind lifted the contact and sent it flying.

It fell to the ground. I think.

Quickly hitting the ground myself, on hands and knees, I went looking for my elusive contact lens. With my left eye closed so my right eye's vision was clearer, I searched through the leaves. And the twigs. And the dirt.

Oh boy…is it on top? Is it underneath? Good grief!

After a fifteen-minute search…nothing. My contact was now forever a part of the Pennsylvania countryside. And I was to ride with only one eye. The truth is, I can't see anything but a bunch of blur without my contact lenses. When you're riding on a road with lots of big bumps and rocks and tree branches, that's not cool at all.

And so it began.

A giant "not cool" moment.

Riding with both eyes opened seemed to do little more than make my right eye…my good eye…totally ineffective at sight, too. My brain couldn't register anything I was seeing with one good eye and one bad eye sharing the workload, but it was able to produce a whole bunch of unbalanced dizziness. I was smart enough to remember that "dizziness" is the warning we receive from our brains before we tip over. This time I listened to the internal voice that implored: *Keep your left eye closed!*

For the next two hours, I did keep my left eye closed. I also pedaled very, very slowly.

Now I had known from the beginning that I should have been more careful taking my contact lens out and putting it in again, but I just plain avoided being careful. I knew every one of the possible consequences beforehand, but I just didn't care to think about any of the cause-and-effect, wind-gust principles that were at play.

Sometimes, we find ourselves in messes…big and small… because we fail to listen to our own internal voice. Without stopping and thinking of the consequences, we take action. Of course, I am a huge proponent of "*taking action*"… but not without thinking first. I don't always succeed in following this rule. However, with a few more one-eyed biking days, I may start succeeding with the "*think first*" thing a bit more.

A lot of the trouble we get ourselves into could be avoided. A lot of the stress we feel every day is because of poorly made decisions and not thinking things through. Remember, life's "gusts" are out there! And when they choose to blow and rise-up, they can affect life events quite significantly.

And if we're not careful, we could find ourselves experiencing a "one-eyed bike riding" day.

EXTRA MILE HERO

Where There Is L.O.V.E.

...there is hope

On September 30, 1972, Daniel and Twinkle Rudberg had planned an evening out with friends in Montreal. They were in their car doing something that happy couples do...talking, sharing, planning, dreaming. As they drove, they had no clue that this would be the last night that any of those activities would ever be shared again. They had no idea that within minutes...because of a bizarre, freak, violent accident...Daniel would die.

The ugly twist of fate that would soon strike the Rudberg's began when they saw a barefoot boy leap from the backseat of a parked car and hurl himself aggressively on an elderly woman. Daniel, seeing the young boy steal the woman's purse, immediately stopped his car and went sprinting after the thief. He caught the 14-year-old purse snatcher, but tragically, Daniel was stabbed. At age 38...within minutes of thinking he was going to be enjoying a great night out...Daniel Rudberg, the Good Samaritan, was dead.

Sometimes life has a way of striking at a moment's notice and changing forever, doesn't it?

Sometimes, too, life seems to make absolutely zero sense.

Not many people would have jumped out of their car to help an assault victim who was a total stranger. In a world where stories abound regarding those who do nothing to help a stranger in immediate distress, Daniel Rudberg was a real hero. In no way should his bold, courageous, and selfless actions have been rewarded with death.

It seems unfathomable.

Thankfully, this tragic story has a happier ending.

It would have been easy to understand if Daniel's wife, Twinkle, would have spent the rest of her life completely scarred by what she witnessed on that 1972 evening. No one would have blamed her if she had faded into a world of bitterness and isolation. But she didn't.

She chose a different path.

With great reason, Twinkle Rudberg was angry at what had happened, certainly. But surprisingly, her anger was not directed at the teenage boy who had wielded the deadly knife. Instead, her anger was directed at all the events that potentially lead a young person to choose to commit a violent act.

During the boy's trial, Twinkle learned that the 14-year-old came from a broken home and had run away to Montreal from the United States. He got caught up in drugs and a violent gang. With a compassion that is truly beyond this world, Twinkle saw the young boy as a victim…just like her husband.

With this profound realization, Twinkle made the decision to give her husbands' death meaning. Despite her gut-wrenching pain, she decided to help other young kids like the boy who killed Daniel.

She decided to create ***L.O.V.E.***

I learned about ***Leave Out Violence*** (*L.O.V.E.*) in New York City. The "big apple" chapter is run by Daniel's daughter, Linda Thibodeau, who was nine years old when her father was murdered. Like Twinkle, her step-mother, Linda is totally immersed in the idea of helping youth, from eleven to eighteen, whose lives have been touched by violence in one form or another. For Linda, "forgiveness" seems a far more powerful direction to head than one of shouting out with anger and ugly bitterness.

"I want to give my dad's death meaning. This is the way to go. This is what makes a difference and helps to potentially prevent the sort of violence that did happen…from happening again. L.O.V.E. helps stop the violence cycle."

The *L.O.V.E.* program is all about communication. It's about creating avenues for kids who have been exposed to violence…as a witness, as a victim, as a perpetrator…a chance to communicate and heal. *L.O.V.E.* creates an opportunity for kids who have been exposed to a world of violent hell, to wash it away with something positive. It focuses on addressing head-on many of the causes of teen violence…isolation, poor mentors, and abuse at home.

And *L.O.V.E.* is spreading.

Since its inception, *L.O.V.E.* has extended from Canada into the United States. It has positively impacted forty thousand teens and is making a mark in New York City schools. It's taking on drugs and gangs. It's addressing bullying and dating violence. It's changing the way kids prone to violence are thinking by creating mental and emotional outlets. *L.O.V.E.* is affecting how kids look at school. It is changing kids' vision of the community and their roles in it. *L.O.V.E.* is creating in individuals the ability to share their view of the world through storytelling and photojournalism, rather than through their fists and weapons.

Sometimes, it's hard to forgive.

Think about all the times that someone's words or actions hurt you personally…and deeply. All of us…in one form or another… hold varying degrees of discomfort when we think about certain people, organizations, or events. Sometimes, it's hard…very, very hard…to let go.

But people like Twinkle and Linda? They have learned to let go in a gigantic way. They have brought meaning to senselessness and are now doing their part to take violence out of the world.

Is the goal impossible? A normal-thinking mind would say it is. History gives us no indication that violence will ever take leave from our earth. But the thousands upon thousands of kids *L.O.V.E.* touches…they have something different to say.

For *L.O.V.E.* kids, there is an alternative to violence. These kids have discovered positive outlets for expression; they have found other…vastly more effective…ways to communicate their hurt and struggle.

And for all of us, that is a very, very good thing.

GEORGE CROSSED HERE

You might not have ever heard of the place, but I know you've seen the famous painting.

The place is Washington Crossing. The illustration depicts George W. (as in Washington not Bush) standing up in a small wooden boat while his soldiers are valiantly rowing. The icy cold river they are crossing looks formidable, but General Washington stands resolute in his mission as the early American flag flies next to him.

Now if you're a history buff, you know that the painting depicts a critical moment in US history: G.W. crossing the Delaware River in the middle of the night on December 25, to attack British troops occupying New Jersey. The year was 1776 and the Brits were proving to be quite feisty about that whole *Declaration of Independence* thing. They had already occupied Boston and New York City, and well, things were looking kinda' bleak for the independence-movement thing we had going on.

General George knew it was paramount that he obtain a significant victory in the war right then. He needed to restore the fighting Americans' faith in their cause and remobilize the spirit of the American people.

On Christmas…when the enemy was partying on the other side…George got dramatic, took a risk and rolled the dice. He roused his tired and cold men…2,000 strong…with a heroic, "Get up and let's go!" and they were off and floating to the other side of the icy Delaware River. Catching the enemy unaware was key.

And with heroic effort, he and his soldiers did, thus changing the course of history.

The attack was a big surprise for the opposing army and the battle concluded with General George taking 900 prisoners. This was the first of several bold actions which changed the momentum of the war. The British soon evacuated New Jersey and...eventually...the United States.

Here I was at the place now called Washington Crossing. I visited the on-sight museum and had my recollection of history refreshed. I was now on the shoreline overlooking the famous river...sitting... gazing...pondering. I was seated where George's men sat before they took off across the river. I was freezing my tail off, but still, I had shoes and a coat, which many of the soldiers did not. Imagine marching through snow and ice with no shoes or coat!

I didn't let the cold bother me too much, though. I was engrossed in sending myself back in history 235+ years. I pictured every detail and thought about what that famous night might have been like. I used my imagination to color in the details.

And as I sat there, I thought about taking risks.

Like George did.

Every one of our days now...has been transformed by Mr. Washington's risk a couple of centuries ago. The course of history was changed when George heroically went against military precedence and attacked...in the middle of a frigid winter night... on Christmas. He took a giant risk, and because he did, he changed American...and world...history.

What happened that night is a great reminder that sometimes... if we want to change the future of our own lives...we need to take bold action...George Washington-like risks. If we don't, we might find ourselves forever sitting on the wrong side of the river, in circumstances that we find undesirable.

Or worse.

We could find ourselves at the end of our lives shaking our heads and muttering, "*If I had only tried....*"

NEW YORK CITY

The Tour included having interview events scheduled in twenty-one cities. From the beginning, however, I was most nervous about the event scheduled in New York City.

Although I currently spend a good portion of my time in the heavily populated Los Angeles area and had spent a month in the Big Apple one summer many years ago, I still find walking in downtown Manhattan a real jolt to my senses. The sky-bound buildings…the barrage of flashing signs…the swell of taxis…the mass of people coming at you and walking with you on the sidewalks…New York City knocks me out of my comfort zone big time.

It's exciting. It's scary. It's intimidating. It's overwhelming.

But I had to be there.

How can you have an event traversing America and leave out the granddaddy of all cities?

I couldn't.

The morning of "New York," Julian and I headed into the city from our Bronx hotel location. We were scheduled to spend the day doing our interviews at *New York Cares* in Manhattan, so we needed to jump in and do the "commute thing" with all the other millions of commuters coming into downtown for the day. Starting at a Bronx subway location, both of us grabbed a handle of our big blue (and heavy!) interview box (complete with photo equipment and other interview-day necessities) and pretended the subway excursion into the city was our "norm."

But of course, it wasn't.

I need to stop right now and say that the New York subway is a man-made miracle. To bring so many people in and out of one place so consistently is truly a great testament to what people can do when faced with an enormous challenge. Bringing a few million people into New York for a day or sending a man to the moon…I don't know which I consider a greater feat.

Once loaded on our train, I looked around the elbow-to-elbow, cramped, standing-room only crowd. The passenger rules seemed simple:

1. Don't talk.
2. Don't smile.
3. Don't make eye contact.

I can assure you, I was not willing to be the only person riding…standing…staring…to break any of the three rules. After quickly observing…and modeling…subway protocol, I adopted the zombie expression and removed all emotion from my face. Driven by a slight tinge of fear, I adapted to the train environment well.

Well almost.

I tried to look straight ahead, but I probably cheated a little as my eyes were glancing everywhere. Riding the New York subway is a visual treat and you have to allow yourself to look around…at least a little.

The vision and thought that I was struck with so powerfully then…and now…is how uniquely different we all are…yet how much we are still all the same. Our sameness includes that we all have basic needs for food, shelter, and love; this reflects our membership in the family of human beings. What makes us all so different, however, is the extraordinarily different approaches we take to getting those things.

There was a suit-and-tie guy reading the *Wall Street Journal*. He might have been Wall Street bound.

There was a young kid with his ear pierced. And his nose. And his lip. With headphones on, he was intent on listening to his music.

A young woman stared intently at the sleeping baby she was

holding. She was probably wishing the baby would stay asleep and not start crying again.

A student artist turned the pages of his sketch pad…obviously reviewing and taking pride in his work.

Another student was studying a huge textbook. It looked like a medical book of some kind.

There was a well-dressed woman wearing walking sneakers… probably her dress shoes for the day were in the bag sitting at her feet.

Two women of middle-eastern origin wore head scarves and had their hands folded in front of them.

A whole family of tourists studied their maps, comparing them to the subway station map on the wall of the train. They were trying hard not to break the no-talk protocol, but sheepishly whispered information back and forth about where to exit.

There were different skin colors and hairstyles. There was a huge variation in clothing…and hats seemed to be a chosen option for a number of people. Body sizes differed vastly. There were lots of briefcases and bags and backpacks. And then there was me and Julian with our big blue container.

All of us subway riders were currently engaged in the same activity…yet each pursuing life in our own unique way.

And that's pretty neat.

We might not always get why a person dresses as she does. We might not understand why someone says what he says. It might be totally beyond us why some people make decisions completely foreign to our thinking. We might not understand some careers, certain hairstyles, or unusual lip piercings.

But that's all okay.

It's what makes the world interesting.

We might all follow suit in our list of basic needs…and we all might even follow a pattern of acting like non-emotional zombies temporarily on a New York subway. But thank goodness for one of the greatest similarities we all share:

Individualism.
And in that similarity, I am glad to be a part.

Journal Entry October 14

Exhausted. Going in and out of the city today really wore me down. The hustle to catch the subway...the long time standing once inside the train...it would be tough doing this every day. You really have to develop a thick skin to live back here. I am happy to get back to the hotel and away from the constant city push. It was a rush. I'm glad it was only for one day.

EXTRA MILE HERO

Arthur Fisher

...home is where the heart is

I met Arthur Fisher in Manhattan at one of the great support organizations in the country, ***New York Cares***. With over 40,000 volunteers in their system, *New York Cares* helps local non-profits by throwing volunteer support to organizations that need a boost in manpower for the purpose of getting something done. The organization shared that Mr. Fisher was one of their true volunteer stand-outs, and I needed to meet him.

When you're a stand-out out in a group of over 40,000, you must be bordering on celebrity fame.

In New York Cares' opinion, Arthur fit that label.

Arthur Fisher was 69 years old when I met him, and as you can imagine with anyone being born in New York City, Arthur has collected his share of memorable experiences and stories. He's seen a lot and led an interesting life. But one thing Arthur has experienced that I hope I never have to live through is being homeless.

In the early 1980s in the largest city in the United States, all of Arthur Fisher's possessions fit into a couple of bags. He was lucky not to have to sleep on the streets. From July 1983 to February 1984, Arthur was a resident at a men's shelter on Park Avenue and 66th Street. There, he shared life...and the world...with a couple of hundred other men, all with varying degrees of saneness.

"We had no privacy. We slept in cots an arm's length away from the next cot. You couldn't trust anybody, either. I had to become friends with two other guys just so we were never one...know what I mean? That kept us three. That kept us safe."

For eight months, homelessness was Arthur's world. For a guy age 43 at the time, this is what his life had come to.

"Living there, it was easy to feel down about yourself. I would ask myself 'Why?' every day. But I knew I was the one that did it…and I knew I was the only one that was going to get me out of it."

Arthur fell into his time of hardship with a series of misfortunes, one after another. First, he lost his job running an IBM computer room in Minnesota. Then he experienced divorce. Next he moved to Chicago hoping to change his luck. There he found a job …but then lost it. Moving to Pennsylvania to be near his family didn't work out, either. So he headed to the place where he started life… a place where he thought he could feel comfortable and secure again…a place he knew. He felt he would once again be able to find his footing there…

In The Big Apple.

"I thought being a native New Yorker, I could do well back at home. But it had changed. It had gotten so much bigger and impersonal…and it was hard to get established like I thought I could."

Whether it was one unlucky decision after another, or whether it was poor decisions made through his own confessed "arrogance," Arthur was running a bad streak that had now extended for nine years.

But he was trying. Hard.

He had always been good at finding a job, and never…never… did he avoid working. Arthur just couldn't find anything that worked out long enough for him to get into a position where money could be saved. After his management job with IBM, he worked as a store clerk and a bartender. He worked at a bowling alley. He cleaned bars after they closed. He was a waiter and a hotel door man. He drove a truck for a clothing company.

"I'd follow a horse with a bucket if it meant work. I didn't care what job it was. I just always needed to work."

Still, he could never get ahead enough financially in order to move out of the shelter.

Until "it" happened.

One day, something extraordinarily bad occurred that really sent Arthur into an immediate "*I need to get out of here fast!*" mode. Sure, there were a number of daily incidents that startled him at first, but he grew used to seeing them, and he learned to be careful. But one particular incident scared him so much that he knew he had to get out.

Now.

"There was a big guy…6'2", 210 pounds or so…and he was always picking on this little guy…maybe 5'7", 140. Well, one day the little guy couldn't take it anymore. He snuck in the bathroom where the big guy was sitting taking care of business, and he went after him with a lead pipe. It was really bad. I knew then I had to get out."

After witnessing the brutal pipe attack, Arthur vowed to do more than just get out of the shelter as soon as possible. He also vowed not to live so selfishly, and he committed to giving something back to the world once he got back on his feet. At that exact moment, he had no specific plan of what he was going to do, but in his own silent "make a deal with God" sort-of-way, Arthur promised to spend his life helping others once he got things right with himself.

It took a few years…almost ten…but Arthur honored his word to God and himself; he started giving back…on October 14, 1995. Sometimes life changing dates are not hard to remember… Arthur, then age 55, joined the volunteer team at *New York Cares*. On that very first day, at 6:15 in the morning in Bryant Park, Arthur was hanging signs in order to direct other volunteers where to go. That day and life moment proved to be such a feel-good event for Arthur, that from then on, he never turned back from a place that finally gave him a set of roots and a real place of belonging.

In *New York Cares*, Arthur Fisher had found his home in helping other people.

As the calendar pages turned, Arthur continued to dedicate himself to the *New York Cares* cause. Soon he found himself leading a once-a-week orientation event for new volunteers...like he once was. A reasonable estimate is that over 15,000 people have gone through Arthur's volunteer-training indoctrination.

That's a lot of societal payback...don't you think?

Arthur's wandering years were tough for him...no doubt...but they also proved to be pivotal years during which life transformation occurred. Arthur Fisher was no longer bitter for what he didn't have. He developed a heart of appreciation for what he did have. He committed his life to serving others...and in the end...that is what Arthur is most grateful for.

Service.

"I know it's easy to feel like a little cog in this great big world...but I know I made a difference. When people come up on the street and say 'I remember you!'...it feels good to know people knew I cared...and I tried."

Arthur is a survivor. He survived job failures. He survived economic crisis. He survived being homeless. He has also survived colon cancer since July 19, 2000.

I asked Arthur, "*So Arthur...do you have a message...a quote...anything that you would call 'Arthur's theme'?*"

With little hesitation, he responded, "*It's from an anonymous source, and it goes like this:*

'I believe in the sun even when it's not shining...
I believe in love even when I am alone...
I believe in God...
even when God is silent.'"

My time with Arthur was humbling. He seemed to accept everything that had ever happened to him as an event that was supposed to have happened. He wasn't frustrated at successes that eluded him. Instead, he was entirely grateful for everything that did come his way. Arthur Fisher seemed to have a great perspective on life:

Never quit. Keep going. Keep being grateful. Keep giving.

Arthur might be a guy who has never had a lot of money in the bank or been famous. But he has found the great joy of planting a tree in downtown New York City, and most of all, he has cheered on 15,000 new volunteers.

Arthur Fisher built a life of great service…and purpose.
And in my book, that's pretty rich living.

TIMEOUT

Ever had a day in which, starting from the very beginning, you just needed to regroup? Some days are like that, huh?

Those are the days when things start out poorly and you just can't get any positive momentum going. On those days, I think it's permissible to take a deep breath, let it out slowly, and shout:

"*Timeout!*"

At least loud enough for you alone to hear.

On October 15th, I had reason to shout "*Timeout!*"

And I took it.

On the 15th, I had intended to get up early and pedal, but coming out of the starting blocks I was instantly stumbling. I hadn't planned on pedaling a great number of miles to begin with, but when I saw the rain...and felt the cold...I knew a late start was in order.

Please get warmer! Please stop raining!

It was a prayer into the Universe that went unheeded. By the end of the day it was evident that the temperature never had increased and the rain never had stopped.

Julian and I finally did get out the door that morning and drove to the point on the bike route where I had stopped pedaling the day before. Meanwhile, I had grown quite comfortable riding in the warm van. Having to open the van door and jump outside in order to prepare for the day's ride was quite a shock. My breath seemed to form its own veil of floating ice when I breathed out, and my cheeks immediately began to sting in the frigid wind.

Only two words could escape from my frozen mouth:

"No way!"

The wind chill factor, although unverified, caused it to feel like 20 below zero. One thing about riding a bike when it's cold and windy, everything is magnified. The chill is fiercely more intense, and the wind seems to take its gusting power up a notch or two when you pedal. Together…bone-chilling cold and stiff winds…are two elements that can turn a bike ride into "*No way!*" fast.

The words "*No way!*" actually turned out to be prophetic as my morning bike ride proved to be extremely short…three minutes covering one half mile short to be exact. Almost immediately upon starting to pedal, I was on my cell phone calling Julian…before he even had time to restart the van.

"*Pick me up!*"

With the riding gear I was currently wearing, it was just too cold to keep going. I jumped into the toasty van as fast as I could to unthaw. And then I got on the phone…to Mom.

Knowing that Mom would be available and near a computer, I asked her to please get on the Internet and look for stores near Norwalk, Connecticut, that might sell winter gear. Yep, I had come full season…starting my ride in the summer and now finishing in the early throes of winter. A top-to-bottom wardrobe change had been overlooked in planning for the event.

Mom hooked me up with a WalMart not too far from where we were. Julian and his immensely reliable navigational ability got us to the parking lot. Shivering, I ran into the store and made my necessary purchases of wind gear, multiple pairs of winter gloves, and a knit cap for ear protection.

I was once again ready to go…back to the day's starting line a second time.

Once decked out, I could pedal much more comfortably. I could still feel the chill's teeth biting through my clothes...but I could handle that. I had to regularly change socks and alternate big-weather gloves over the rest of the day's ride because of the rain, but it was all manageable.

Before re-gearing? It was impossible.

Of course, the day proved to be long....and slow...and wet... and cold. In fact, it was so cold that it started to actually snow by the end of the day's ride. Overall though, covering thirty miles in such crummy weather wasn't too bad. I was proud of my effort.

I didn't quit.

Quitting is always an option when things seem impossible. A better choice, however, is to simply take a step back...re-evaluate our approach...and see what "tools" might be needed to get past the failing part...and move on to the succeeding part.

If we are going to make an effort to do a job...any job...why not give the job our very best effort? Doesn't it make sense that if we are going to put forth energy to do "something" that we should also give ourselves the greatest possible chance of succeeding at that "something"?

Just going through the motions for the sake of going through the motions doesn't cut it for me. If doing our best, succeeding and feeling great about our effort isn't really a high priority, we can always climb back into the proverbial warm van with a cup of hot chocolate and just watch it rain.

Right?

But really, is that what will make us feel good in the long run? Is that what we really want?

I don't think so.

EXTRA MILE HERO

Madye Magic

...a battery charger of the human spirit

Dr. Madye Henson has a special gift.

It is a gift that disarms a fellow conversationalist into a feeling that you have known her for years. It is a gift that allows someone leaving her company to feel positively charged. It is a gift, in my opinion, that she shares with some of the most charismatic people who have ever graced the human stage.

When you sit with Madye, you are her priority. Nothing distracts her gaze; nothing sidelines her thought; nothing hijacks her total presence in being in the moment with you. Along the way in your conversation with her, you will probably sense she is a listener...a motivator...a cheerleader...a coach...a leader...and a people-builder.

She is all of those things.

It's easy to feel Madye cares from the moment she meets you. Her eyes and smile unwaveringly lock onto yours. Her energy is totally positive and, when she shakes your hand, she holds on to it for what seems an extra second...almost as if she is trying to determine just what kind of "positive charge" she needs to pass on to you. In conversation, her interest is sincere and her questions have depth. She wants to know you. She wants to add positive energy to your world. She wants that chance to clap for you. She wants to discover how she can leave you feeling that your path is clearer, your resolve is stronger, or your courage is up one more notch.

Because that's what Madye Henson does.

She supports people. She empowers people. She leaves people feeling charged up. She helps people believe that all things are possible. And in my mind, that's a special gift.

I have a title for people like Madye. To me, it is a far more elite and impressive title than *Executive Director, President, CEO* or the like. This title, though, is not a job title; it's a "human being" title.

Madye Henson…in my book…is a *Battery Charger of the Human Spirit.*

What exactly is a *Battery Charger of the Human Spirit*?

It is my term for a person dedicated to charging the "life battery" of another person. Think of an unwilling car whose battery has run out of juice and won't start. No matter how many times you turn the key in the ignition, there is just no connection or charge. The car sits there…dead. In order to get the car running again, the temporarily unmoving car needs to be connected via battery cables with a car whose engine is purring.

And then…once the connection has been made and the charge applied…"Vroom!"

Now apply that same principle to people.

Take a person who feels beaten down by life or afraid to move forward; connect him or her to a *Battery Charger of the Human Spirit.* What will happen is a restoration of confidence, strength, will, and energy. The *Battery Charger* offers the encouragement that lifts a temporarily defeated soul up from the ranks of the defeated. The charged up person provides an extra dose of courage to push a little harder in the effort to reach a desired goal. The *Battery Charger* empowers another to dig deeper, push harder, not give up…and, to go for it. *Battery Chargers of the Human Spirit* help other people maximize the potential…of a moment…and a lifetime. They encourage others to live at their highest mental, emotional, spiritual, and physical level.

When you consider a title like that, it's easy to understand why no job title could ever be as important. And in the specific case of Madye, the *Battery Charger of the Human Spirit* label fits her as perfectly as a designer dress fits a Hollywood starlet walking down the Red Carpet on Oscar night.

Except Madye wears her label 365 days a year.

A quick walk into Madye's life history reveals how the mold of her character took shape and how she grew into her title. Her parents were great believers in supporting and encouraging others. They would consistently open their St. Louis home to friends and family when Madye was growing up, and if someone was temporarily down on their luck, the "*Welcome*" sign was flashing. It was early in life…at home…where she learned to step forward in order to support and serve. It was also at home where she learned "*sharing was the thing to do*."

In addition to teaching her the values of service and giving to others, Madye's parents treated her with a second powerful life lesson: believe in yourself. With a mom an educator and a dad an entrepreneur, Madye received a double dose of what it meant to carry both a positive mindset and a resourceful spirit. She and her three brothers grew up believing that the power to achieve what they wanted in life was within their grasp if they wanted it badly enough.

But Madye's home education was not yet complete.

Certainly the seeds of support and service had been deeply rooted into Madye's conscious, but her grandfather added one final life lesson: develop a civic voice. It was his love of history and his deep passion for justice and human rights that really shined a light on how Madye could perhaps best apply her lessons of supporting and serving. Shared history lessons showed Madye that a single person's effort can positively affect the course of events; one voice can make a difference. The inspirational seed of dedicating one's self to civic-oriented activities in order to make a positive impact on the world was planted.

Over the course of Madye's lifetime, she has stayed true to the lessons her parents and grandfather taught. She has dedicated her life to service.

"My passion and my life is civic service," Madye says. *"I have always sought out ways to make a difference and get involved."*

When Madye sees a need to help people, an opportunity to serve, a hole that needs to be filled...she responds. In 1986, she saw a need for young inner-city kids to get a perspective of what life could be like in a major corporate environment, so she created the non-profit, *Ace It*. In 1995, she became a school board member in St. Louis. In 1999, she became a licensed minister. In 2003, she created a non-profit, the *Urban School Leadership Consortium*, designed to bring urban school leaders together to make a difference. In 2006, Madye became Vice President of Community Impact Development for *United Way Worldwide*. And in 2008, Madye Henson became the leader of one of Washington, DC's most dynamic non-profit organizations...***Greater DC Cares.***

Sitting a mere five blocks from the White House, *Greater DC Cares* filters volunteers into the welcoming arms of one of the 750 non-profits the organization serves. During the first eighteen months of her leadership, Madye catapulted the volunteer force from 5,000 to 24,000 volunteers.

Again, that's just what Madye does. She fires up people and organizations in regards to their potential. She throws her all into making a difference.

Madye always remembers her roots. With her, it's not cliché. When she writes her name, it's right there...*Madye Grovetta Jean Henson*. "Madye" was her father's mother. "Grovetta" was after her father, Grover. "Jean" was her mother's mother. They are all a part of her. And so are the early lessons.

In 1968, Madye was severely burned and was required to stay in the hospital. She happened to be there on April 4th. Being only nine years old, she wasn't really sure what was happening on this tragic day in history, but many of the doctors and nurses in the hospital were extremely distraught. She asked her parents why.

"*Dr. Martin Luther King was killed today,*" her parents told her. She then told her mom and dad:

"He must have been doing something great to make such an impact. I want to do something that makes an impact on people, too."

And she has ever since.

For all of her years, Madye Grovetta Jean Henson has been spreading her "*Madye Magic.*" With eyes always on the bigger picture, with heart always dedicated to serving, Madye has woven herself into positions that make a difference in people's lives. Her "*Welcome*" sign for new opportunities to be of value is always posted. And in all those years of giving and encouraging, she has earned her *Battery Charger of the Human Spirit* title.

In a follow-up phone conversation with Madye after our initial meeting, she quoted to me a Martin Luther King verse she lives by:

"Everybody can be great...because everybody can serve."

In a world where fame, wealth and power are desired by so many of us, it is nice to be directed back to a higher purpose.

And that, too, is what Madye does.

She directs us back to our own roots...and the deep seated knowledge within each of us that *it is better to give than to take.*

Madye Henson is a reminder to me that the real value of life is not found looking in the mirror wondering what I can do to make my own life better. Rather, it is found looking out the window to see what I can do to make other people's lives better.

"Madye Magic?" Yes...it's powerful. And...yes...she has it. And...yes...it is difference-making.

But let's not forget that the magic...the lives transformed because of her efforts...are results of the fact that she embodies the title *Battery Charger of the Human Spirit.*

And as we take a reflective moment to look at our own lives individually, maybe we, too, might aspire to such a grand title. If we did, I guarantee that the world would be a much different place.

SOME PEOPLE

Once in a while, all the internal peace in the world still isn't enough to protect you from *some people.*

Who are *some people*?

They are the ones whose agenda seems to center on finding an unusual sort of happiness by causing others to experience the opposite. When you're riding a bicycle across the country, these people are more specifically identified as the spitters, the "shoulder" drivers who attempt to scare you, the aluminum can throwers…you get the idea.

It doesn't matter how much you may have been smiling before you meet *some people*…it's often difficult to retain your smile mojo after encountering one of them. I am not certain what joy *some people* find in making the world a bit uglier…but all we can do is to keep on pedaling.

My worst encounter with *some people* was a total oddity. It was in Stoney Creek, Connecticut. Now Stoney Creek is about as rural and country as it comes. The roads are beautiful and the scenery certainly holds its own with any place in the country that I have seen. The anchors of a modern society seem to hold far less appeal; they just don't seem as important out here.

The area is very lightly populated. Trucks are far more popular than any new model of a high-end luxury car, so it seemed very unusual that a limo would pull up to the small mom-and-pop country store near where I was resting. The limo looked out of place.

A very drunk younger guy stumbled out of the limo and along with him…a six-pack of empty beer cans was thrown outside to litter the ground. It was obviously a celebration of some sort…perhaps a bachelor party that had just started to find its drunken stride.

When you pedal a bike from California to Connecticut, one thing that you deeply appreciate is the beauty of nature. At the same time, however, you become witness to the horrible stain man inflicts upon nature by insensitively throwing his garbage everywhere so freely. It's inconceivable to me how *some people* can be so callous as to roll down a window and just throw out their cans and food bags.

It's ugly.

Well, on this day…when I saw it being done…I couldn't accept it. A country full of beer can polluters had taken their toll on this rider, and it was time for action.

I dashed over to the limo to address the polluting scoundrels. In drunken disbelief, the partygoers watched me pick up their garbage and add it back into the mess that was already in the limo's backseat.

Wise or not, I had to do what I had to do.

Of course, my action was met by a flurry of slurred words. Recognizing only a few of the words because of the uniqueness of their use, I questioned either their education or my lack of one for not knowing how all those words fit together in a coherent sentence.

My comments back to them sparked more words…and then the "cans really hit the fan." An empty twelve-pack came flying toward me.

The limo driver, recognizing that confrontation was clearly in sight, turned on the car and hit the gas. With passengers screaming and garbage flying out the window, the limo driver sped away.

Maybe the driver was thinking that he was only paid to get the limo back safely. But I think he missed the much bigger picture. He just let his customers do as they pleased and litter the countryside.

When wrong happens, and our world is touched negatively by *some people,* we have a choice. We can chose to turn our heads or not… to let injustice occur and to turn our voices mute or not.

What is the big-picture choice?

What makes the world a better place?

There will come a time for each of us …probably sooner rather than later…when we will be touched by *some people.* And when that time arrives, the choice of how to respond will be promoted to front and center.

Do we turn our heads…or not?

For me? I hope I always pick up the littered can.

And hand it back.

Journal Entry October 17:
The daylight hours are getting shorter, and I finished the ride today in total darkness. Julian had to drive closely behind me so that the van's lights could shine on the road in front of me and I could see. Finally, we reached our day's Niantic, Connecticut, destination and my constant hollering back to Julian "How much further?" ended.

THE ATLANTIC

The day had to come sooner or later. For me it arrived 93 days after the *Extra Mile America Tour* began.

I reached the other ocean.

The exact place where I would stop my trip was never pre-determined...but I knew it was to be somewhere near Boston. On October 22, I dipped my front tire into the Atlantic at Sandy Beach in Cohassett, Massachusetts.

This became my someplace near Boston.

The temperature had been dropping daily and, mentally, I knew it was time to put this long ride to an end. Physically I was spent. Enough was enough!

Around noon that day, I told Julian:

"*It's time. I'm touching water today.*"

How did I feel when it finally happened? How did I feel after pedaling a bicycle from one ocean to the other? I was numb.

Here I was with my bike out on a windy Atlantic beach...Julian was videotaping the grand finale...but I was numb. I didn't feel that amazing, ecstatic exhilaration that one might have expected to feel after succeeding in riding a bike nearly 4,000 miles.

Oddly, I felt the opposite.

While pushing my bike's front tire into the ocean water, I felt a surge of melancholy. Emotionally, I wished that the cross-country ride wasn't over. I didn't want to load my bike for the last time. I didn't want it to end, because after accomplishing any big goal, the question pops up:

"Now what?"

This was a "*Now what?*" moment.

That's what it's like sometimes…isn't it? After we accomplish the big goal we had set our sights on, we are left feeling:

"Okay…what do I do now?"

There can be a natural letdown.

Having big goals…goals that inspire us individually…are undoubtedly important and beneficial. They give our lives purpose. They make life adventurous, exciting, and passionate. When we don't have one of those big goals to shoot for, it feels like riding a bike with a flat tire.

Life seems slower, harder, and more tedious.

Dipping my tire into the Atlantic Ocean was not nearly as thrilling and as motivating to my spirit as dipping my back tire into the Pacific Ocean when I began. It just wasn't.

You know what this tells me?

That the real "juice" of life is not in achieving the goal; it's in setting goals and the journey toward fulfilling the dream. That's the part where we get to truly experience feeling alive.

And that's also where we discover the true greatness within ourselves.

Journal Entry October 22:
As I looked for a landing place to finish, the coolest thing happened. I was in downtown Cohasset looking for a road down to the ocean. I was having trouble finding where to go when I asked a woman sitting on a park bench…reading: "How do I get to the ocean?" I told her my story…and she got so excited to share in the adventure…that she packed her two kids into the car and the three of them escorted me to the water!

EXTRA MILE HERO

Magical Moments
...and Friends For Tomorrow

Diane Lesneski Auger's destiny was determined on one special day.

She was in high school and she was a "barn rat." Hearing the term initially, I would have sworn a barn rat was the arch nemesis that every barn cat was encouraged to hunt. But in the big city of Boston, I was given a lesson in proper "barn rat" terminology.

"Barn rats" are people who love horses and will do everything they can to be around them. Grooming them, feeding them, walking them, cleaning messy stalls...to a barn rat none of this is a big deal. They love it all.

And that describes Diane.

It seems that somewhere along the path of growing-up, all little girls fall in love with ponies and horses. But with most little girls, the horse dream fades because of a family's circumstances and ability to have and care for one. When one is lucky enough to live on or near a ranch, as in Diane's case, the love of horses is fostered and allowed to continue to grow.

And when that happens, the love of horses continues forever.

But it wasn't only Diane's love of horses that changed her life. It's the miracle she witnessed firsthand by seeing what being around horses can do for people.

"When I was a teenager, I saw a young boy...around twelve... approach the horse he had been spending time on. The boy had never been able to communicate with words until one special day when he got next to his horse's face and whispered 'thank you.' Seeing something like that changes a person's life."

With that small whisper, Diane's future…with horses…was forever determined.

In 1994, Diane started ***Friends For Tomorrow***, a therapeutic horseback riding program to help physically and emotionally challenged children. Soliciting the donation of a single horse, a riding site, and discounted board and feed, Diane began her program with just three riding participants. Today, the program has grown from that single borrowed horse to a flourishing and well-respected program that serves forty-four students annually…with a significant waiting list.

In her program, each young rider becomes friends with a special horse. The young rider learns to groom, lead, and ride. Each session involves a unique team that consists of the child rider, an instructor, and one, two or three volunteers depending on the seriousness of the rider's handicap.

The reason there is a waiting list is because of what transpires in her program. Parents witness miraculous changes in their kids. They boast that their child's self-confidence is raised….muscles, flexibility, balance, and posture are enhanced and strengthened… communication attempts are increased…and the young rider's mind and body explode with an experience that connects them to the world in a deeply moving fashion.

"There is something wonderfully spiritual about horses. They seem to be able to read emotional states in people in a very special way. Developmentally challenged children seem to thrive around horses. The setting can be magical.

"I remember a young boy who started with us at age six. He was petite and shy, and he was unable to walk by himself. We would lift young Nicky up on the horse, and he would literally crumble on the saddle because of not having enough strength to sit there alone. As the years passed, however, Nicky became stronger and more confident…and everything about his mental and physical make-up changed. After being with the program for thirteen years, Nicky is achieving a dream that at one time might have seemed impossible. He is going to college."

When I was growing up, my greatest companion was my dog, Heather. She was a sable Shetland Sheepdog with a docked tail and a couple of toes missing on her back foot. Shortly after her birth, a mother dog who also had a litter of puppies thought Heather was hers and tried to drag her through the fence. When my parents asked me which Sheltie we should buy, the choice was obvious. My heart went out to the little one who had experienced her early months in a hard way. After that day, Heather and I were inseparable. The bond we established was so significant that I still miss her a great deal, and it has been thirty years since her eyes said their last good-bye.

Some animals have a very special quality about them. They have an ability to connect and communicate in a way that is hard to explain. If you have ever been sad, needing a friend, and had a pet look up at you with understanding eyes, you know what I mean.

This is what I think the kids of *Friends For Tomorrow* experience on Diane's horses. This is what the young twelve-year-old boy felt when he communicated his first whisper to a horse over twenty years ago. This is what Nicky experienced as he found the strength to build a life of normalcy. This is what Diane feels every time she puts one of her students on a horse.

They feel a phenomenal connection.

Some moments in life are pretty darn magical. Some experiences are flat-out unexplainable.

Like a boy on a horse.

And one with a dog.

THE LAST DAY

Boston.
City #21.
The end of the *Extra Mile America Tour.*

An early morning cancellation from the Executive Director of the ***Ronald McDonald House*** took my interview group down to the smallest of any city; but today, it was okay.

It was the final city. It was the final day. And I was ready to go home.

The last person I shared time with was Barbara Salisbury, the CEO of ***MAB Community Services***, the oldest social service agency in the country that provides services to the blind. Barbara was a very insightful woman who had led an extraordinary life. She had been the State Budget Director in Massachusetts, an Assistant Dean at Harvard, and now she was taking her new…yet very old…organization to the next step of growth and development by expanding and providing residential and vocational programs for people with developmental disabilities.

I took the liberty of relaxing during this last interview, and the time I spent with Barbara was as long as any I shared with one person on the Tour. Talking to Barbara about Boston politics and the future of the *extra mile message* was interesting. Her insights were engaging, and our conversation was the transition I needed before packing up and walking out the door of my last meeting room on the Tour.

After an hour together talking, it was finally time to go.

Julian and I loaded all of our equipment and materials for the very last time. It was too cold…and too late in the day…to do much Boston site seeing, so with a quick clothes change at the van, we piled in and headed west.

The ride back to California had begun.

The great *extra-mile adventure*, which—including preparations—had encompassed nearly eleven months of my life...was over. Altogether, a dozen people had been involved with me directly, helping to put on the *Extra Mile America Tour*. Dozens of others across the country had played their roles...big and small.

It had been a monster-sized commitment.

And it was finished.

As we headed out of Boston, I saw a sign indicating that a childhood home of former President John F. Kennedy was nearby. Julian and I pointed the van in that direction.

As we pulled up in front of the house, I imagined the young future president playing in the yard. I imagined him walking through the neighborhood with all sorts of interesting thoughts spinning through his young mind. I could see him walking up the steps into the house and heading to the family dinner table. I imagined his young life.

Putting myself back a number of decades, I realized that right there in that very neighborhood...the "past" had once been the "present." Different residents now occupied the homes in this historic neighborhood, but years and years ago, there was a young boy full of ideas, and with a whole future ahead of him, who would go on to occupy the most powerful seat in world government. But today, the same street holds only the memory of the great history that once was unfolding right there under the trees.

Many times on the *Extra Mile America Tour* I had been in a hurry to end my adventure. On the hard days, on the disappointing days, the sick days, and the cold days...on none of those days could the ride and Tour get over quickly enough for me.

But while sitting in the van in front of JFK's childhood house, I was reminded that we should never really wish too hard for the days to fly by, and for events to end...because they will all end soon enough. It doesn't matter if you are a future President of the United States playing in your childhood neighborhood, or just a determined guy pedaling a bike across America trying to make a motivational difference...someday, the events of life end for each of us.

San Francisco to Boston on a bike?

What a great and amazing adventure!

The chance to experience all of the good days...and bad days... of life?

An even greater adventure!

BELIEVE, ENERGY, TIME

I have never had the ambition to review my route and recalculate the exact number of miles I actually pedaled. I'll tell you, though, after driving the lengthy distance from Boston back to California on a basically straight line...without all the zigging and zagging up and down the map like I did on the bike...it's a long way across this country.

Even riding in the van back to Sacramento, the total number of miles seemed unreal. Of course, the six days it took to return home were nothing compared to the 93 days it took to get there.

Once the Tour ended, I couldn't get back fast enough. With a foot on the gas, Julian and I drove Interstate 80 most of the way home. Gone were all the detours and side roads. Gone, too, was the up-close and personal view of practically every inch of road I'd previously pedaled.

On average, we knocked off about five hundred miles a day on our return. I chose to do the majority of the driving homeward because the focused activity allowed me to limit my excessive dwelling on the now finished *Extra Mile America Tour*.

I'm a thinker, and I love to dissect events from top to bottom once they are completed. Now, though, I felt like cutting myself some slack. Having invested so much time and money on this adventure, I didn't want to beat myself up right away over a list of "*I should haves.*"

By only a couple hours we missed a huge snowstorm that walloped Denver and the Rockies. Snow and slush were gathering fast, and I was concerned that without snow chains, we weren't getting over the mountains...but we got lucky and crossed over just in time. After beating the mountain-country snowstorm, we sailed through Utah, Nevada, and the rest of the way.

As I got used to being home again, I had plenty of time to reflect and think about what had been accomplished. The ocean-to-ocean pedal, the support from big city mayors, the amazing people I met and interviewed, the coordinated events in 21 cities, over seventy media interviews, the 22 different cities and states that had proclaimed November 1, 2009 "*Extra Mile Day*"...the logistics had been incredible and a lot had been achieved.

As I write this now, though, I believe that one of the greatest successes of the *Extra Mile America Tour* is something that is unlisted above. It is something internal...and has everything to do with cementing into the very core of my being three key concepts:

1. If you BELIEVE in yourself or an idea with enough internal force, you can mold and shape the future into whatever your aspirations may be.
2. If you apply whole-hearted and passionate ENERGY into an endeavor, you will find exciting results.
3. If you let TIME work its magic, great things can be built.

BELIEVE. ENERGY. TIME.

I learned to B.E.T. on myself.

When we BET on ourselves, life takes on a self-determined, invigorating direction and remarkable results can be produced. When we BET on ourselves, an invisible idea can be turned into a visible reality. When we BET on ourselves, we transform our lives into something fulfilling, purposeful, and difference-making.

When we BET on ourselves, we live up to our very highest potential.

And really, can you think of anything better to do with your life than to live up to YOUR own potential?

I can think of nothing more inspiring.

Journal Entry November 5:
I presented 95-year-old Raynia Kinniston the first Extra Mile America Award. It was a surprise ceremony at Mercy Hospital and over twenty Raynia fans were in attendance. When she realized why I was really there...to present her with a $1,000 check...Raynia looked up at me and with the most kind, appreciative, and disbelieving eyes, she kept saying over and over, "I can't believe this. I can't believe this." Rocking Raynia's world tonight was one of the best feelings I have ever experienced.

EXTRA MILE DAY

The following cities and states declared November 1, 2009, "*Extra Mile Day*" with a resolution or proclamation:

Arizona - State Senator Amanda Aguirre

Casper, Wyoming - Mayor Kenyne Schlager

Chesapeake, Virginia - Mayor Alan Krasnoff

Cincinnati, Ohio - Mayor Mark Mallory

Columbus, Ohio - Mayor Michael B. Coleman

Dublin, Ohio - Mayor Marilee Chinnici-Zuercher

Fayetteville, Arkansas - Mayor Lioneld Jordan

Fort Wayne, Indiana - Mayor Tom Henry

Hawaii - State Senator Suzanne Chun Oakland
State Representative Karen Awana

Honolulu, Hawaii - Councilmember Ikaika Anderson

Houston, Texas - Councilmember Pam Holm

Jacksonville, Florida - Mayor John Peyton

Lewiston, Maine - Mayor Larry Gilbert

Little Rock, Arkansas - Mayor Mark Stodola

Montgomery, Alabama - Mayor Todd Strange

Nampa, Idaho - Mayor Tom Dale

Paterson, New Jersey - Mayor Jose Torres

Rockford, Illinois - Mayor Lawrence Morrissey

Sacramento, California - Mayor Kevin Johnson

San Jose, California - Councilmember Sam Liccardo

Seattle, Washington - Council President Richard Conlin

Tucson, Arizona - Councilmember Rodney Glassman

Warwick, Rhode Island - Mayor Scott Avedisian

AMAZING EXTRA MILE AMERICANS

interviewed during the Extra Mile America Tour

Angelo Adams is a member of the Mt. Hope Corps at **Mt. Hope Learning Center** (RI), which provides a safe environment for children and adults to learn skills that will give them more productive futures. Angelo is one of seven children born to a single mom who was incarcerated, leaving him and his siblings in foster care. Angelo mentors youth, works with gang members to help them change their lives, and mediates neighborhood conflicts. (www.mthopelearningcenter.org)

Denise Aiken works for **Rhode Island Legal Services**, the state's major law firm for low-income people with civil legal problems. The organization seek to ensure that low-income people have food, shelter, income, medical care, and freedom from domestic violence. (www.rils.org)

Afshan Ajmiri is an **AmeriCorps** member who helps low-income seniors in high school prepare for college. As a College Guide, Afshan helps students and their families navigate the financial aid process and provides academic advising and support. (www.americorps.gov)

Roy Alexander is the CEO of **Sacramento Children's Home** (CA), an organization that has provided a host of programs and services to help abused or at-risk children, as well as families in crisis, for over 140 years. (www.kidshome.org)

Brooke Allen is a self-proclaimed "volunteer-aholic." As a project leader for **Greater Philadelphia Cares** she tutors children, leads arts and crafts enrichment classes, and coordinates activities for the kids at a transitional housing facility. In 2008, she and her boyfriend Matt started Building Blox, a community clean-up program, and they also work with Friends of Triangle Park on a beautification project. Brooke also volunteers with Associated Services for the Blind to assist clients on their shopping trips. (www.philacares.com)

As of 2009, **Herb Anderson** had served on the Board of Directors of **United Way Allen County** (IN) for 12 years. He is a leader on labor issues, and he helped raise $4.5 million for the workplace campaign. Because of his leadership, 60-70% of the workers at the BF Goodrich tire plant where he works are involved in some capacity with United Way Allen County. (www.unitedwayallencounty.org)

Pamela Atkinson works with **Volunteers of America, Utah**, spending much of her time moving between legislative hearings, community boards, and public speaking duties, and she has worked tirelessly toward policy changes that help the homeless. She also rides on the Homeless Street Outreach van every week. (www.voaut.org)

Diane Auger was a "barn rat" working the horse stalls in high school. She heard a 12-year-old disabled boy who had never communicated with words whisper "thank you" to a horse after riding. That experience caused her to start **Friends For Tomorrow** (Lincoln, MA), a therapeutic horse riding program for children and adults with disabilities. (www.friendsfortomorrow.org)

Gary Bagley is the Executive Director of **New York Cares**, and played a part in growing their volunteer base by 60%—from 27,000 to 43,000 volunteers. (www.newyorkcares.org)

Nicole Bailey is the Arts and Crafts Leader at **Camp Hobé** (Salt Lake City, UT), a summer camp geared to creating a fun and positive environment for children with cancer and their siblings. Camp Hobé allows the kids the chance to just be kids away from the confines of a hospital. (www.camphobekids.org)

Mitch Ball, a remarkable young man, was diagnosed with Duchenne Muscular Dystrophy (DMD) at age 4. Although bound to a wheelchair with a ventilator to breathe, he keeps a positive attitude and created video blogs to open people's eyes to what it's like living with a disability. (www.mitchballsworld.blogspot.com)

Carl Bartholome is the Assistant Vice President of Wells Fargo and a volunteer at **Winners Circle** (Omaha, NE), an organization that encourages and rewards student achievement through a program of goal-setting and celebrating accomplishments. Volunteer "Goal Buddies" visit classrooms to support and motivate students, as well as reward them with medals during Winners Circle celebrations. (www.winners-circle.org)

Tom Baxter is the Executive Director of **Friends of the Riverfront**, which was started in 1992 to reclaim Pittsburgh's riverfronts for public access and greenway/recreational use. Tom's work helps protect and restore the city's rivers and expand water and land trails. Friends of the Riverfront has been involved in creating nearly all of the trails along Pittsburgh's shores. (www.friendsoftheriverfront.org)

Dotti Bechtol is Executive Director of **Health Hope Network** (Pittsburgh, PA), which runs the Stroke Survivor Connection program. This program provides free, weekly therapy support groups for stroke survivors and their caregivers. As a caretaker and breast cancer survivor herself, Dotti is deeply sensitive to the plight of stroke victims and their families. (www.healthhopenetwork.org)

Christina Beckwith is the Executive Director of **Camp Hobé** (Salt Lake City, UT), a summer camp geared to creating a fun and positive environment for children with cancer and their siblings. Camp Hobé allows the kids the chance to just be kids away from the confines of a hospital. (www.camphobekids.org)

Brad and Libby Birky are a husband-wife team who quit their jobs to start **S.A.M.E. (So All May Eat) Café** (Denver, CO), a restaurant with no prices on the menu. S.A.M.E. Café serves anyone and everyone in the community, regardless of their ability to pay. If a patron cannot afford to pay for their meal, they are encouraged to volunteer their time at the restaurant. (www.soallmayeat.org)

Roxanne Black started **Friends' Health Connection** (New Brunswick, NJ), an organization that connects individuals with similar health conditions for mutual support. Roxanne was diagnosed with lupus at age 15, and her personal experience was the inspiration for this organization, which she started in her college dorm room. (www.48friend.org)

Monique Bourdage is the Project Director of **Girls Rock Denver** (CO), a summer camp that empowers girls by giving them music instruction, encouraging self-expression and self-esteem, and providing a nonjudgmental space that promotes creativity. Monique also teaches basic skills at a nonprofit that helps low-income single parents obtain employment and self-sufficiency. (www.girlsrockdenver.org)

Joyce Bourgault is the Executive Director of **Helping Hands Health & Wellness Center**, a faith-based, free clinic that serves adult, low-income individuals in the greater Columbus, Ohio, area who do not have health insurance. The free clinic provides health care, health education, medical referrals, social service, and spiritual guidance. (www.ascension-columbus.org/pages.asp?pageid=48891)

Sean Brady is the Assistant Executive Director of **Venture Outdoors** (PA), an organization that encourages Pittsburgh residents to participate in outdoor recreational activities and promotes Pittsburgh's unique natural amenities. Venture Outdoors also seeks to foster a greater appreciation for the environment and inspire people to live an active lifestyle. (www.ventureoutdoors.org)

Charles H. Britt is the Founder and Chairman of the **Center for Minority Achievement in Science and Technology (CMAST)**. He was compelled to create the organization in response to ongoing reports and statistics citing the poor academic achievement of minority students. CMAST (Washington, DC), expands educational opportunities to increase minority enrollment, retention, and graduation rates. (www.cmast.org)

Nichole Brown volunteers at **Willow House** (Riverwoods, IL), an organization that is dedicated to helping children and families who are grieving. Willow House began in 1998, when a small group of bereavement professionals began meeting with those in need in the living room of the founder. Nichole helps provide a safe place of hope where it is okay to feel sad and talk about it, and memories of loved ones are invited and respected. (www.willowhouse.org)

Tracey Brummett works for **Challenge Denver** (CO), which aims to improve the climate at middle and high schools by eliminating teasing and violence, and inspiring students to become positive forces in their communities. Challenge Day is a day-long workshop that promotes self-acceptance and respect for others, and is followed by Youth Engagement Sessions to instill these values. (www.challengedenver.org)

Paul Bryant is the Executive Director of UMCC Wesley House and a volunteer at **Winners Circle** (Omaha, NE), an organization that encourages and rewards student achievement through a program of goal-setting and celebrating accomplishments. Volunteer "Goal Buddies" visit classrooms to support and motivate students, as well as reward them with medals during Winners Circle celebrations. (www.winners-circle.org)

Philip Buffum is an **AmeriCorps** member who helps low-income seniors in high school prepare for college. He teaches SAT prep classes and FAFSA workshops nights and weekends. (www.americorps.gov)

Pat Burritt, the volunteer manager of the **Sacramento Fire Department Community Emergency Response Team** (CERT), schedules all CERT trainings, drills, classes, and community service events. She also spent many weeks volunteering with the Red Cross to assist the victims of Hurricane Katrina. (www.sacramentocert.net)

Thom Cassidy is a logistics associate at **Veterans Green Jobs**, an organization that provides green jobs education and career opportunities for veterans. Thom served in the Army from 2001-2005, graduated from Veterans Green Jobs Academy (Denver, CO) and focuses his efforts on community organizing and social justice. (www.veteransgreenjobs.org)

Tiela Chalmers works for the **San Francisco Bar Association's Volunteer Legal Services Program**. In addition to maintaining and motivating volunteer lawyers from the city's top law firms, the program has collaborated with the California DMV to provide homeless individuals with the state identification cards they need to apply for many benefits and services. (www.sfbar.org/volunteer)

Angie Champion founded **H.O.P.E., INC. (Healing Others by Promoting Enrichment)**, an organization that provides community-based mentoring, matching families that practice positive, spiritually based parenting with at-risk youth and single parent families in need of a support system. Angie hopes to not only provide assistance to families, but also to break down the barriers and stereo-types that exist in diverse communities. (Omaha, NE), (www.hopeincorporated.org)

Marlon Cifuentes works for **English For Action** (Providence, RI), which serves Latino families through English language and childcare programs that link language, learning, leadership development, and community-building. English For Action uses innovative learning tools, such as the visual arts, theater of the oppressed, and action projects to engage learners. (www.englishforaction.org)

Stephanie Clark founded **My Daughter's Keeper** (North Brunswick, NJ), which provides support and resources to mothers/caregivers and their daughters to help strengthen their relationships. Through her organization, mothers and daughters comes together to identify solutions to problems such as communication, peer pressure, and teen pregnancy. (www.mydaughterskeeper.org)

Ted Cochran received the "gift of life" by way of a kidney transplant. At age 28, his mother donated one of her kidneys so that he could have a healthier life after being diagnosed with chronic renal failure. A year later, he founded

My Angel Foundation (Des Moines, IA), to honor his mother's gift, help other transplant patients and their families, and advocate for the very thing that saved his life—organ donation. (www.myangelfoundation.org)

Jodi Cooper is the Community Coordinator of **inCommon Community Development**, a faith-based organization that fights poverty by cultivating community networks. InCommon holistically develops vulnerable neighborhoods and populations, such as the impoverished in downtown Omaha, the Park Avenue neighborhood, and the Burundian refugee population. Their goal is to transform communities *through* community. (www.incommoncd.org)

When **Anita Croce** was diagnosed with Benign Essential Blepharospasm (BEB), a condition that caused her to be blinded by her eyelids, she decided to help others who are suffering from the same condition. In 1986, she formed a support group for residents of Ohio; in 2009, she presided over 11 states as the North Central District Director of the **BEB Research Foundation**. She holds support meetings and international conferences in Columbus, and provides support and referrals for others with BEB. (www.blepharospasm.org)

Natasha Cross is the President and CEO of **EYE (Engaging Youth Entrepreneurs) for Change** (Baltimore, MD), an organization that empowers and prepares youth to become competitive in a global economy through entrepreneurial skill building, financial literacy, and leadership. Natasha hopes to teach young people that entrepreneurship is just as viable a career option as any other. (www.eyeforchange.org)

Jennifer and Brian Daly helped start **The Matthews Foundation** to provide financial assistance to families of children who have been diagnosed with leukemia. The foundation is named after their son and another young boy, both named Matthew, who were both diagnosed with leukemia in 2006. (www.matthewsfoundation.org)

Christopher Darby, at 24 years old, was the youngest person on the **Mosaic Project**'s Board of Directors in 2009. The Mosaic Project (Oakland, CA), brings together children of diverse backgrounds through outdoor school and youth leadership programs, while teaching them to appreciate diversity and empowering them to work toward peace. (www.mosaicproject.org)

Frank Darling is the president of the California chapter of **Guitars Not Guns**, an organization based in Peachtree, GA, that aims to reduce violence and self-destructive behavior among at-risk children by providing them with guitars and music lessons. (www.guitarsnotguns.org)

Brian Dean is the Executive Director of **Jersey Cares**, which in 2009 had a volunteer database of over 10,000 individuals. Jersey Cares has monthly calendar projects, such as Hunger Helpers, Stepping with Seniors, and Caring Closet, as well as a corporate service program and leadership opportunities. (www.jerseycares.org)

Rosaura and **Aurora De la Cruz** are sisters who volunteer with **Desert Ministries** (Omaha, NE), a volunteer organization that arranges weekly visits to the elderly in nursing homes. Desert Ministries values the life and wisdom of the elderly and seeks to bring "hope through love" to nursing home residents. (www.desertministries.org)

Mindy Derr is the Founder and Executive Director of **Fore Hope** (Columbus, OH), a therapeutic golf program that was Mindy was inspired to start after her father was diagnosed with Lou Gehrig's disease. Mindy's organization allows individuals affected by disease and disability to get back on the golf course. (www.forehope.org)

Aisha Desince provides villages in Sierra Leone with basic potable water supply systems through the organization **Khadarlis for Sierra Leone**. Khadarlis also implements solar electricity, health education and infection control programs. Through programs that encourage agricultural efficiency, this Providence, RI, organization help villagers become self-reliant. (www.khadarlis.org)

Ivy Devlin works for **Project Homeless Connect** (San Francisco, CA) through the Sprint Corporation, connecting individuals with their family and friends at phone call tables, looking up phone numbers with scant remembered information, and doing whatever it takes to have a connection take place. (www.projecthomelessconnect.com)

Jon Dewey is in charge of the **Salt Lake City Police Department's Operation Safe Passage** for Bonneville Elementary School. Operation Safe Passage volunteers ensure the safety of children walking to and from school by deterring criminal activity and protecting children from potential dangers like abductions, drug dealers, and bullies. (www.slcpd.com/getinvolved/operationsafepassage.html)

Al and **Germaine Dietsch** are a husband and wife team who founded **Spellbinders**(Denver, CO) an organization that is restoring the art of oral storytelling to enhance literacy and create connections between elders and youth. Al and Germaine have trained over 1,000 volunteers nationally, and in 2008 alone, volunteers attended over 2,000 classrooms.

Rebecca Drobnick is the Coordinator of **Operation Home Front Ohio**, an organization that provides emergency assistance and morale to U.S. troops, their families, and wounded veterans. They also help children and spouses stay in touch with their loved ones and offer financial assistance during family crises. (www.operationhomefront.net/ohio)

Marne Dunn, a volunteer at **Women's Empowerment**, built a computer-training program so that homeless women can learn the technology skills needed to return to the workplace. She has developed the organization's computer lab and organized the all-volunteer teaching crew of Intel staff members. (www.womens-empowerment.org)

Judy Eakin is the Executive Director of **HEARTH** (Pittsburgh, PA) which provides transi-tional housing to homeless women with children and permanent supportive housing for women with a mental health or physical disability. Judy's work equips women with skills in communication, problem-solving, and decision making, and helps them reconnect to their community. (www.hearth-bp.org)

Teresa Elder is the Chief Flight Nurse for **Flight For Life Colorado**, the first hospital-based medical helicopter program in the nation. Teresa jumps on board the helicopter and races out to life-or-death situations to provide critical care support. (www.flightforlifecolorado.org)

Jennifer Emmert brings the love and companionship of animals to people in healthcare facilities, libraries, and schools, through the **San Francisco Society for the Prevention of Cruelty to Animals' Animal Assisted Therapy Program.** (www.sfspca.org/programs-services/animal-assisted-therapy)

Leo "Mr. Diggs" Endres teaches the members of **Boys and Girls Club of Greater Sacramento** how to harvest vegetables as part of the Club Garden program. Since Mr. Diggs started volunteering, the club has seen as an increase in youth participation, and the kids use the products of the garden in nutrition and cooking classes. (www.bgcsac.org)

Murat Eskicioglu and his team at SMG Corporation provide **Project Homeless Connect** (San Francisco, CA) with a venue, tables & chairs, audio/visual equipment, internet connectivity, set-up and tear-down labor, and sandwiches for 3,000 people. (www.projecthomelessconnect.com)

Paul Falkowski is the Executive Director of **Desert Ministries** (Omaha, NE) a volunteer organization that arranges weekly visits to the elderly in nursing homes. Desert Ministries values the life and wisdom of the elderly and seeks to bring "hope through love" to nursing home residents. (www.desertministries.org)

Al Finnical is a multi-faceted volunteer at **Habitat for Humanity Greater Columbus.** In the span of one year, he volunteered as a crew lead, construction support volunteer, photographer, speaker's bureau volunteer, and budget mentor. He also leads workshops on how to improve credit scores for homeowners who were rejected from the program due to poor credit history. (www.habitatcolumbus.org)

Ellen Firestone is the Senior Finance & Communications Executive of **Greater Philadelphia Cares.** Ellen oversees the organization's Finance, Communications, and Involvement divisions, and was instrumental in improving the organization's Reading STARS program—a literacy program for children. (www.philacares.com)

Dr. Jeffrey Fishberger is on the Board of Directors of **The Trevor Project,** a nonprofit established to promote the acceptance of lesbian, gay, bisexual, transgender, and questioning youth, and to aid in suicide prevention among that group. Dr. Fishberger has trained helpline counselors and facilitated workshops for homeless LGBT youth and young people living with HIV/AIDS. (www.thetrevorproject.org)

As of 2009, **Arthur Fisher** had been a volunteer at **New York Cares** for 15 years, serving more than 800 hours. He leads projects and has also been a speaker, having oriented thousands of people since he started. (www.newyorkcares.org)

Shannon Foley is the Executive Director of **Love Hope Strength Foundation**, a music-centered cancer charity dedicated to providing support for cancer centers around the world. Shannon has organized concerts on Mount Everest and the Empire State Building to raise funds for medical equipment and mobile cancer units in places like Nepal, Peru, and sub-saharan Africa. (www.lovehopestrength.org)

Suaz Forsythe started working for **Animal Friends**, a full-service community resource center committed to nurturing the human-animal bond, in 1996. She helped create a program to support and sustain rabbit adoptions. Animal Friends started during World War II, when a group of Pittsburgh, Pennsylvania, citizens came together in an effort to find homes for soldiers' pets when they left for war. (www.thinkingoutsidethecage.org)

William Fuellenbach is the Executive Director of **Northern Nevada HOPES**, an outpatient program that is dedicated to improving the lives of those affected by HIV/AIDS. HOPES provides a variety of services including counseling, clinical services, housing assistance, and education. (www.nnhopes.org)

Shirley Fuertes works for **English For Action,** (Providence, RI) which serves Latino families through English language and childcare programs that link language, learning, leadership development, and community-building. English For Action uses innovative learning tools such as the visual arts, theater of the oppressed, and action projects to engage learners. (www.englishforaction.org)

Rod Gardner is the Sales and Marketing Associate at **The Douglas Center** (Stokie, IL) a day program that offers a wide variety of services for individuals with severe developmental disabilities. The Douglas Center provides a work program, developmental rehabilitation, vocational skills training, and a seniors program. Their mission is to help individuals manage their disabilities, build self-esteem, and improve independent living skills. (www.thedouglascenter.com)

Mary Gebhard is a volunteer Airport Ambassador at **Fort Wayne International Airport**. She greets visitors with a warm welcome upon their arrival, and has stayed long after her volunteer shift to assist travelers who had transportation problems.

Jon Gelleta is an AmeriCorps member in the Corporate Service Department of **Jersey Cares**. He is also a volunteer EMT with the South Orange Rescue Squad, where he works 12-hour shifts. He leads other volunteers in serving meals to the homeless every month and sketches murals that brighten shelters, schools, and community centers. (www.jerseycares.org)

Jenn Gibbons is the Founder and Coach of **Recovery on Water** (Chicago, IL) a rowing team that gives breast cancer survivors the opportunity to become active in their recovery and gain support from fellow survivors. Jenn rowed at Michigan State University and is a US Rowing Level II Certified Coach. (www.recoveryonwater.org)

Tim Gibson has volunteered more than 1,000 hours with **New York Cares** from 2007 to 2009. He is a team leader for projects ranging from Meal Service to serving people with disabilities. www.newyorkcares.org)

Gannon Gillespie is the Director of U.S. Operations at **Tostan**, which empowers African communities to bring about sustainable development and positive social transformation based on respect for human rights. Since 1991, Tostan has brought holistic 30-month education programs to 10 African countries. These programs promote community empowerment and democracy, enhance economic opportunities, and protect maternal and child health. (www.tostan.org)

Kevin Good is the Founder and Director of **Acts 4 Youth (A4Y)**, which motivates at-risk boys toward character, competence, and career development. A4Y (Baltimore, MD) places adult male role models with boys in a small-group setting to teach critical thinking, communication, conflict resolution, goal setting, and business planning. (www.acts4youth.com)

Susan Gross founded **One Village at a Time** (Boston, MA) after taking a trip to Ethiopia in 2002. Her organization strives to create small, sustainable programs for AIDS orphans and their villages in Africa. Susan focuses on feeding, educating, and nurturing the children, while empowering the local leadership, church leadership, and local businesses to support the community. (www.onevillageatatime.org)

Willie Grove serves on the Board of Directors of the **Columbus Zoological Park Association** and the Board of Trustees of **Opera Columbus.** He brought the two organizations together when he suggested a summer concert event: Go Wild! For Opera at the Columbus Zoo and Aquarium. As of 2009, the Ohio event has raised $200,000 for the two organizations, and Willie has dedicated 1,300 hours of service. (www.operacolumbus.org/productions)

Peter Hanink is a member of the Board of the **Disaster Accountability Project**, which monitors the public accountability of the US disaster prevention and response systems and engages stakeholders in tracking recommendations for their improvement. The project was inspired by frustration over the botched response after Hurricane Katrina, and now demands accountability. (www.disasteraccountability.com)

Mike Hannigan is the Co-Founder of **Give Something Back Business Products**, an independent office supply company that, as of 2009, had given away 82% of its profits to charity. Over a period of 18 years, Give

Something Back contributed $4 million to impact local communities. (www.givesomethingback.com)

Rachel Harvey volunteers for **Book 'Em** (Pittsburgh, PA) a project that sends hundreds of packages of books and resource guides to prisoners. Book 'Em aims to reduce prisoners' feelings of isolation, assist them in their self-education, and counteract the dehumanizing effects of the prison system.(www.thomasmertoncenter.org/bookem)

Tom Heinz is the Founder and Executive Director of **East Bay Innovations** which provides support to enable individuals with developmental disabilities to live on their own, work in a job they enjoy, and participate fully in community life (CA). In 2005, Tom won The Bill Rosenberg Memorial Award from Cal-TASH, which is presented to individuals who exhibit leadership in promoting the inclusion of persons with severe disabilities. (www.eastbayinnovations.com)

Liz Henderson is the Volunteer Coordinator at **Seniors Helping Others**, (southern Rhode Island) which helps senior citizen volunteers give back through programs such as Meals on Wheels, Visitation to the Homebound, and Mobile Library Delivery Services. (www.southernrivol.org)

Dr. Madye Henson is the Executive Director of **Greater DC Cares**, and was formerly the vice president of community impact at United Way of America. As of 2009, her organization was capable of mobilizing 13,000 DC volunteers to assist over 750 local and area non-profits. (www.greaterdccares.org)

Tracy Henson participates in **Volunteers of America, Utah** through the Marriott Vacation Club Team. Tracy organizes her team members for food donation drives and has rallied the support of the senior managers of her corporate team. (www.voaut.org)

Joan Hicks (Wilmington, DE) has dedicated thousands of hours of volunteer service in her lifetime. She first started volunteering in 1998 at **Alfred I. DuPont Hospital for Children**, and in 2009, she volunteered in 8 different departments. She also serves on the board of **Sojourner's Place**, a homeless shelter where she runs meetings for the women. In addition, she has adopted a highway and picks up trash four times a week. (www.nemours.org/waystogive/volunteer.html)

George Hill is a volunteer dactylographer (a fingerprint expert), recording and submitting data for the **Fort Wayne Police Department** (IN) and **Allen County Sheriff Department**. He was one of 8 volunteers to successfully complete the 40-hour FBI training when the program first started in 1994. (www.fwpd.org, www.allencountysheriff.com)

Andrew Hoffman is the Executive Director of **NeighborLink Fort Wayne**, a grassroots, web-based organization that connects volunteers with homeowners who need assistance with home maintenance and repairs. Anyone can seek free assistance by posting a project on the NeighborLink website, and volunteers can register to help out with a project of their choosing. (www.neighborlinkfortwayne.org)

Christie Holderegger is the VP & Chief Development & Communications Officer at **Volunteers of America Greater Sacramento & Northern Nevada.** VOA is the home of Operation Backpack, a program that provides backpacks, school supplies, and other services to homeless children and families. (www.voa-sac.org/Events/OperationBackpack/tabid/2119/Default.aspx)

Sheila Holzworth (Des Moines, IA) is an internationally known athlete who has climbed Mount Rainier, won national and international competitions in downhill skiing, water skiing, and trick skiing, and has ridden a tandem bike across the state of Iowa. She also happens to be 100% blind, the result of an accident that happened when she was 10 years old.

Herb and **Jan Hoover** are a retired couple who have volunteered with **UC Davis Health System** for over a decade. They install medical devices in phones that allow a person in distress to easily call 9-1-1 and reach emergency personnel. (www.ucdmc.ucdavis.edu)

Regina Jackson is the Executive Director of **East Oakland Youth Development Center**, an organization that encourages youth to become self-sufficient, responsible members of their community and offers a variety of services and activities. Regina has received the Fannie Lou Hamer Emerging Leader Award from UC Berkeley and The Jefferson Award for Community Service. (www.eoydc.org)

John Jerger served as a Peace Corps volunteer in Thailand, where he worked on Information and Communications Technology and taught computer skills to rural elementary school students. He volunteers at **Chicago Cares** to write a computer curriculum resource, at Lakeview Pantry to assist in planning a fundraiser, and with the Northside Anti-Hunger Network to help submit a grant for a fellowship. (www.chicagocares.org)

Dee Johnson provides villages in Sierra Leone with basic potable water supply systems through the organization **Khadarlis for Sierra Leone.** Khadarlis (Providence, RI) also implements solar electricity, health education and infection control programs. Through programs that encourage agricultural efficiency, this organization helps villagers become self-reliant. (www.khadarlis.org)

Kelly and **Jim Jolkowski** (Omaha, NE) started **Project Jason** after their son disappeared without a trace from their driveway. They now dedicate themselves fully to providing resources and support to other families who have experienced a family member disappearing. (www.projectjason.org)

Claire Jones is the Program Manager for the **Health Federation of Philadelphia**'s smoking cessation program. HFP's Smoking Cessation Counselors offer group smoking cessation programs and individual follow-up for patients who are ready to stop or reduce their use of tobacco products. (www.healthfederation.org)

Renae Jones is the Happy Bear Program Coordinator at **Blank Children's Hospital** (Des Moines, IA). The program teaches young children how to recognize and resist sexual abuse, thereby protecting them from such experiences. The program is run and managed entirely by Renae, and incredible volunteers bring Happy Bear to life. (www.blankchildrens.org)

Jo Kaufman brings the love and companionship of animals to people in healthcare facilities, libraries, and schools, through the **San Francisco Society for the Prevention of Cruelty to Animals' Animal Assisted Therapy Program.** (www.sfspca.org/programs-services/animal-assisted-therapy)

Lori Keys is the Executive Director of **Aboite New Trails** (Fort Wayne, IN) the area's leader in advocacy, fundraising, and building of pedestrian and bicycle facilities. As of 2009, Lori's organization had built 14.5 miles of new trails over four years. (www.aboitenewtrails.org)

Raynia Kinniston is a 95-year-old woman who, in 2009, had volunteered at **Mercy General Hospital**, Sacramento, for 49 years. Three days a week, Raynia catches the bus and a train to get to the hospital. (www.mercygeneral.org)

Carolyn Kohn is the Founder of **The Brady Kohn Foundation** (Wilmington, DE) an organization with a dual mission to educate the public about the potential of stem cells from umbilical cord blood and to fund non-embryonic stem cell research. The organization honors Brady Kohn, Carolyn's son, who passed away at 3 years old from complications from aplastic anemia. (www.thebradykohnfoundation.org)

Emily Lampert is a volunteer tutor and mentor for **Let's Get Ready** at Columbia University, in Harlem and in White Plains, New York. Let's Get Ready expands access to college in America by mobilizing and equipping a movement of college students to help high school students get into college. Emily provides underprivileged students with intensive SAT preparation, college advising, and a role model. (www.letsgetready.org)

Isaac Langford is the Executive Director of the **National Homeless Protection Agency**, which assists the homeless through drug treatment programs, domestic abuse counseling, housing application services, and shelter referrals. Issac's goal is to protect the rights of the homeless within the US, and his organization reports anyone who mistreats the homeless. (www.homelessprotection.webs.com)

Carylynn Larson was inspired to start **Rock Recovery** (Arlington, VA) an organization that helps individuals overcome food and exercise addiction, after struggling with these issues herself throughout her life. Rock Recovery provides faith-based therapy and support, while allowing residents to remain engaged in their daily activities, such as work and school. (www.rockrecovery.net)

Effie Marie Lascarides is the Founder and President of **Alzheimer's CURE Foundation** (Providence, RI) an organization that is raising $20 million to be awarded to the scientist(s) who find a cure for Alzheimer's. The foundation provides scholarships and creates awareness through community outreach programs, informational sessions, and health fairs. Through her work, Effie is helping to accelerate a cure for Alzheimer's. (www.alzcure.org)

Ruth Leacock started **Computers For Africa**, an organization that, as of 2009, has sent over 1800 refurbished computers to Africa. The mission of her (NE) organization is to promote sustainable Information and Communications Technology development in rural communities. (www.computers4africa.org.uk)

Ray Lian is an Organizer for **Stop Modern Slavery**, which educates the DC area community about human trafficking and fosters grassroots movements to combat modern slavery. Ray participates in Stop Modern Slavery's three-person action teams to collaborate with NGOs, government, business, and the community. (www.stopmodernslavery.org)

Matthew Linzer is the Ecology Instructor for **Oakland Leaf**'s "Love Cultivating Schoolyards" program, which promotes nutrition, sustainability, and creative education for Oakland's youth. The long-term goal of this project is to facilitate secure food sources and micro-enterprises based on the products yielded from urban gardens. (www.oaklandleaf.org)

Megan Low works for the **San Francisco Bar Association's Volunteer Legal Services Program.** In addition to maintaining and motivating volunteer lawyers from the city's top law firms, the program has collaborated with the California DMV to provide homeless individuals with the state identification cards they need to apply for many benefits and services. (preview.sfbar.org/volunteer)

Nancy Lublin is the "Chief Old Person" of ***Do Something***, an organization that inspires young people to believe that change is possible, and trains, funds, and mobilizes them to be leaders in their communities. Nancy has led the effort to award grant money to young people who want to make a difference, and also founded the organization ***Dress for Success***, which provides women with career development training. (www.dosomething.org, www.dressforsuccess.org)

Vicky Luckett is the Program Director at **Magnolia Women's Recovery Program, Inc.** (Hayward, CA), an organization that assists pregnant women and new mothers in recovering from substance abuse addictions, while healing them emotionally and spiritually as well. Vicky provides case management support services for an average of forty-five clients a month. (www.magnoliarecovery.org)

Becky Mack is a volunteer at St. John's Shelter and Project Leader of "**Project Birthday**" (Sacramento, CA), which provides birthday parties for children living in homeless shelters and transitional housing facilities. Though she is a single mom with a full-time job, as of 2009 she had logged in over three thousand volunteer hours. (www.projectbirthday.org)

Roger Macker, a retired math teacher with decades of teaching experience, volunteers his time as a tutor at **Sacramento Food Bank & Family Services.** He contributed over six hundred volunteer hours within two years. (www.sfbs.org)

Kendall Massett is the President of **The Brady Kohn Foundation** (DE), an organization with a dual mission to educate the public about the potential of stem cells from umbilical cord blood and to fund non-embryonic stem cell research. The organization honors Brady Kohn, the founder's son, who passed away at 3 years old from complications from aplastic anemia. (www.thebradykohnfoundation.org)

Marget Maurer is the Executive Director of **Project Create** (DC) bringing professionally-led arts experiences to children living in emergency, transitional, and long-term affordable housing programs. Margaret's organization empowers kids to reach their potential by fostering critical thinking skills, creative expression, self-esteem, and social skills. (www.projectcreatedc.org)

Jonathan Mawhinney is an 18-year-old race car driver who raised money for **The Wall Youth Foundation** through his Pennies From Heaven Penny Drive. The Wall Youth Center (CA) provides afterschool services for students in 6th through 12th grade. (www.thewallcarmichael.com/mawhinneys-penny-drive.html)

Gene Mayhew was the original Chairman of the **National MS Society Delaware Chapter**'s Bike to the Bay event from 1982 to 1997. He expanded the event, which raises money for research and assistance for individuals with multiple sclerosis, from 22 riders to over 1,300 riders. As of 2009, the Delaware Chapter has raised over $1.3 million for research and programs. (www.nationalmssociety.org/ded)

Bill Maynard oversees the **Fremont Community Garden** in Sacramento and has worked on a wide variety of volunteer projects related to gardening, food access, community building, and beautification. He has turned blighted lots into "urban green spaces," organized free farmers markets for low-income community members, and helped Hmong families who were gardening in toxic drainage canals find a safe location to garden. (www.cadanet.org/fcg)

Thomas McCaugherty, the V.P. of CTCI Wiring, started volunteering with **Jersey Cares** in 2007. He spearheaded Stepping Stones in East Orange, a male mentoring program that teaches job and life skills to young men. He also founded Angel Initiatives Incorporated to provide financial support to young people striving to become successful. Thomas provided Project Home in Jersey City with a backyard makeover, supplying landscaping professionals and brand new equipment and toys for the residents. (www.jerseycares.org)

Andrew McKnight is the Executive Director of **The Challenge Program** (Wilmington, DE), an organization that offers a Construction Training Program for out-of-school youth ages eighteen to twenty-one. Trainees enrolled in the program complete 700 hours of site-based construction training and educational work while working toward their GED, thereby providing educational opportunities to students with barriers to employability. (www.challengeprogram.org)

Candice Metzler volunteers on the Homeless Youth Street Outreach Team of **Volunteers of America, Utah**. She has led her own team of volunteers and organized an eight-campus food and donation drive. She advocates for the homeless by speaking at town hall meetings and hosting presentations at the public library. (www.voaut.org)

Alan Michel is the Director and Co-Founder of **HOME, Inc. (Here-in Our Motives Evolve)**, which teaches video production and media analysis to educators and youth to foster confident, creative individuals. Alan's work allows students to develop creative media projects while teaching them to effectively evaluate media messages. (www.homeinc.org)

Matt Migliore is a self-proclaimed "volunteer-aholic." As a project leader for **Greater Philadelphia Cares**, he tutors children, leads arts and crafts enrichment classes, and coordinates activities for the kids at a transitional housing facility. In 2008, he and his girlfriend Brooke started Building Blox, a community clean-up program, and they also work with Friends of Triangle Park on a beautification project. (www.philacares.com)

Parker Mills is an Americorps service member at **HandsOn Hartford** (CT), and weekly volunteer at MANNA House soup kitchen. He also joined volunteers painting murals and sports silhouettes in school gymnasiums and auditoriums, added hop-scotch and four square elements to the playground, and built bookcases, benches, and chalkboards. (www.handsonhartford.org)

Sarah Miretti is the Assistant Director of Development at **New Jersey SEEDS**, an academic enrichment and leadership development program for high-achieving, low-income youth. NJ SEEDS seeks to prepare qualified students for placement at top schools and empower students to live lives of leadership, professional accomplishment, and service to the community. (www.njseeds.org)

Kinga Misiarz works for **Challenge Denver**, which aims to improve the climate at middle and high schools, eliminating teasing and violence, and inspiring students to become positive forces in their communities. Challenge Day, a day-long workshop, promotes self-acceptance and respect for others, and is followed by Youth Engagement Sessions to instill these values. (www.challengedenver.org)

Dr. Mark Mitchell is the President and Founder of **Connecticut Coalition for Environmental Justice**, an organization that protects urban environments by promoting individual, corporate, and governmental responsibility. Mark's work is focused on eliminating discriminatory policies for production or storage of environmental toxins and preventing and reducing environmentally associated harmful health effects. (www.environmental-justice.org)

Wilfredo Molina is a volunteer with Oakland Leaf's "Love Cultivating Schoolyards" program, which promotes nutrition, sustainability, and creative education for Oakland's youth. The long-term goal of this project is to facilitate secure food sources and micro-enterprises based on the products yielded from urban gardens. (www.oaklandleaf.org)

Jena Munson is the Therapeutic Recreation Lead at **Alegent Health Immanuel Rehabilitation Center**'s Sports and Leisure Program (Omaha, NE). The program sponsors golf, soccer, volleyball, bowling and softball for individuals with disabilities, thereby improving their self-confidence and sense of belonging (NE, IA). (www.alegent.com/rehab)

Anne Murr is the Coordinator of **Drake University's Adult Literacy Center** (Des Moines, IA), which provides one-on-one tutoring for adults. The majority of the center's students are employed in jobs that require only basic reading skills, but they are eager to learn—Anne's work helps them fulfill their job, school, and home responsibilities. (www.drake.edu/soe/projects/adult_lit_center.php)

Julian Nagler is a high school student and member of Sacramento's Youth Commission who helped found the **VIBE Urban Youth Lounge and Career Center,** a peer-to-peer resource center that will provide tutoring, job skills training, and opportunities for service projects. (www.thevibefoundation.org)

Craig Newmark, founder of Craigslist, has teamed up with **AllForGood.org** to encourage people to respond to President Obama's call to service by seeking out volunteer opportunities in their area. (www.allforgood.org)

Stephanie Nilva is the Executive Director of **Day One**, an organization that partners with New York City youth to end dating abuse and domestic violence through community education, support services, legal advocacy, and leadership development. Since 2003, Day One has educated thousands of youth about how to identify and maintain healthy relationships, obtain legal protection when necessary, and assist others experiencing abuse. (www.dayoneny.org)

Jeanette Obal serves patients and families affected by ALS (amyotrophic lateral sclerosis), or Lou Gehrig's disease, through **ALS in the Heartland**. This (Omaha, NE) organization provides equipment such as wheelchairs and walkers at no charge, respite care, and support groups for patients, families, and friends. (www.alsintheheartland.org)

Ije Obilo is the Director of Volunteer Programs at **Jersey Cares** (NJ) and has been volunteering since the age of 11, when she attended a medical mission trip to Nigeria with her family. She volunteers countless hours with the Nigerian Healthcare Foundation based in New Jersey, whose mission is to conduct free medical services, combat the spread of disease, and improve healthcare conditions within the Nigerian population. She also works with the Youth Advocate Programs of Essex County to ensure that young people who have been incarcerated have positive alternatives. (www.jerseycares.org)

Emily Orologio was a finalist for the Comcast SportsNet 2009 All-Star Teacher Award for her excellent work as a first-year teacher. She went the extra mile for her students by providing free notebooks to those who could not afford them, and by giving out her personal cell phone number so that her students could call for homework help.

Brighid O'Shaughnessy is the Founder of **Erasing the Distance,** a group of (IL) artists and mental health advocates who create professional theatrical productions based on true stories about mental illness. Their goal is to create awareness of mental illness, disarm stigma, and provide a safe forum for discussions about mental health. Brighid received DePaul University's David O. Justice Award for her use of theatre to educate about mental illness. (www.erasingthedistance.org)

Lisa Osmond is a leading spokesperson for **Yes Utah!**, an organ donor registry program. Her son Adam came home from school one day after learning about organ donation, and said, "Mom…if something happens to me, will you make sure my organs are donated?" A few weeks later, Adam died. Lisa honored Adam's request and turned it into a life-changing mission. (www.yesutah.org)

Bob and **Pat Parks** have informally adopted the **Volunteers of America, Utah's Center for Women and Children**, a residential detoxification center for homeless women and children. They lead a weekly spiritual group that is a powerful part of the women's recovery from substance abuse, and they bring in a large group every weekend to sing to the women at the center. They have organized many drives at their church and hold barbecues for the women in the warmer months. (www.voaut.org)

Ami Patel is a site supervisor for the Reading STARS program at **Greater Philadelphia Cares**. Reading STARS is a literacy program where volunteers work one-on-one with students to boost their reading abilities. Ami coordinated 200 city employees who volunteered as coaches in hopes of increasing literacy rates in Philadelphia's public school system. (www.phila.com/stars.htm)

Tom Patrick is the Volunteer Manager at **Moveable Feast** (Baltimore, MD) a meal delivery program for homebound people living with AIDS and women undergoing treatment for breast cancer. Moveable Feast recognizes that people with AIDS and other life-challenging conditions cannot always provide adequate meals for themselves, so they provide meals and nutritional counseling to those in need. (www.mfeast.org)

Fred Patterson started the **Partners and Learners (PALS)** tutoring program at one of Denver Public Schools' highest-need schools. PALS volunteers meet with a student for weekly tutoring sessions to teach them that high expectations, sacrifice, hard work, and believing in yourself will create success. (http://cpc.dpsk12.org)

Rich Philips is the Community Relations Coordinator of **PAWS for People**, an organization with hundreds of volunteers who take their own pets to facilities within the community to provide affection, cheer, and comfort. PAWS visits facilities such as those for disabled children, seniors living with Alzheimer's, and chemotherapy patients (DE, MD, PA, NJ). (www.pawsforpeople.org)

Kursten Pickup is the Coordinator of **Refugee Youth Project**, an afterschool program run by Baltimore City Community College in conjunction with local refugee resettlement agencies. Refugee Youth Project seeks to improve the lives of

Baltimore's youngest refugees by supporting their academic needs, and making their acculturation simple and meaningful. (www.refugeeyouthproject.org)

Bill and **Marlou Pieper** are volunteers at **Mentor Iowa**, an organization that trains mentors to work with abused, neglected, and delinquent children who are under the jurisdiction of the Juvenile Court. Bill and Marlou mentor two young African refugees, going above and beyond by spending much more than the average amount of time (which is usually six hours per month) with their mentees. (www.mentoriowa.org)

Sally Pitts-Rakes is the Program Coordinator of **Students Overseeing Students** (**SOS**), a peer mentoring and tutoring program for students who are held back in eighth grade due to low scores on the Delaware Student Testing Program test. As of 2009, Sally has recruited and trained High School Preparation Assistants who have mentored and tutored over a hundred students. (http://sos-peermentoring-tutoring-ai.webs.com/)

Mary Quinet is a volunteer tutor at **Drake University's Adult Literacy Center** (Des Moines, IA) which provides one-on-one tutoring sessions for adult learners. The majority of the center's students are employed in jobs that require only basic reading skills, but they are eager to learn from tutors like Mary. (www.drake.edu/soe/projects/adult_lit_center.php)

April Raczka is the Sexual Assault Crisis Services Director at **YWCA of New Britain** (CT). SACS offers free, confidential service for victims of sexual assault, including crisis counseling, prevention education programs, confidential hotlines, and support groups. April's work is critical in helping victims and their families regain feelings of independence, optimism, and hope. (www.ywcanewbritain.org, www.connsacs.org)

Joe Ramos volunteers his photography skills with **Project Homeless Connect** (San Francisco, CA), taking individual black & white portraits of the clients. Joe's work treats each with dignity and humanity. He prints and mails the photos to every individual with a mailing address. (www.projecthomelessconnect.com)

Lynne Robinson is the Executive Director of **PAWS for People**, an organization with hundreds of volunteers who take their own pets to facilities within the community to provide affection, cheer, and comfort. PAWS visits facilities such as those for disabled children, seniors living with Alzheimer's, and chemotherapy patients (DE, MD, PA, NJ). (www.pawsforpeople.org)

Adam Rosenberg is the Executive Director of the **Baltimore Child Abuse Center** (**BCAC**), an organization that exists to prevent children who have been sexually abused from being re-victimized by a lengthy investigative process. In addition to providing treatment and counseling, BCAC has developed a coordinated response with local authorities that has resulted in timely, child-sensitive investigations of child sexual abuse. (www.baltimorechildabusecenter.org)

Marilyn Rossetti is the Executive Director of **Hartford Areas Rally Together (HART)**, which uses community organizing as a means of increasing citizen empowerment and participation in events affecting their lives. HART holds public officials accountable to the citizens they represent, and has campaigns focused on immigrant rights and quality of life in Hartford neighborhoods. (www.hartofhartford.org)

Bill Roth is the Chief Advancement Officer of **Mount St. Vincent Home** (Denver, CO), which provides services and programs for residents up to the eighth grade who are coping with emotional and behavioral problems. Roth, known as "Coach" to many of the residents, has created numerous athletic programs and ensured that every child who comes to Mount St. Vincent receives their very own bicycle. (www.msvhome.org)

Jody Ruggiero is the Founder and President of **Tune In To Kids**, an organization that promotes media literacy, reading, and parent-child involvement. Jody's organization put on an amazing free family support day that was attended by ten thousand people in Reno, Nevada. (www.tuneintokids.org)

Lisa Russell is one of three founders of **The Matthews Foundation** (Bel Air, MD), which provides financial assistance to families of children who have been diagnosed with leukemia. Lisa witnessed her father-in-law battle the disease, so she joined forces with others who were also affected in order to make a difference. (www.matthewsfoundation.org)

Barbara Salisbury is the CEO of **MAB Community Services**, the oldest social service agency in the country providing services to individuals who are blind or visually impaired. In the 1970s, MAB created some of Massachusetts' first community-based residential and vocational programs for adults with developmental disabilities. (www.mabcommunity.org)

Sabrina Schalley serves patients and families affected by ALS (amyotrophic lateral sclerosis), or Lou Gehrig's disease, through **ALS in the Heartland** (Omaha, NE), This organization provides equipment such as wheelchairs and walkers at no charge, respite care, and support groups for patients, families, and friends. (www.alsintheheartland.org)

David Schenirer is a high school student and member of Sacramento's Youth Commission who helped found the **VIBE Urban Youth Lounge and Career Center**, a peer-to-peer resource center that will provide tutoring, job skills training, and opportunities for service projects. (www.thevibefoundation.org)

Jerusha Schulze is a program coordinator for **NJLEEP (New Jersey Law and Education Empowerment Project)**, tutoring and mentoring local high school students with a pre-law curriculum program. She also coordinates a project at Goodwill Rescue Mission, serving meals to over a hundred local residents. She organizes and distributes donations for women and children at Caring Closets and coordinates fundraising efforts for American Cancer Society. (www.njleep.org)

Martin Schwartz is the President of **Vehicles for Change**, a community initiative that accepts donated cars and provides them for low-income families (DC, MD, VA). Seventy-three percent of car donation recipients obtained better jobs within a year, and 94% were able to take their children to after-school, athletic, and community activities never before possible. Martin's organization has awarded over three thousand cars as of 2009, enabling recipients to get on the road to self-sufficiency. (www.vehiclesforchange.org)

Liz Segovis works for **Rhode Island Legal Services**, the state's major law firm for low-income people with civil legal problems. The organization seeks to ensure that low-income people have food, shelter, income, medical care, and freedom from domestic violence. (www.rils.org)

Bill Serovy volunteers with **Alzheimer's CURE Foundation**, an organization that is raising twenty million dollars to be awarded to the scientist(s) who find a cure for Alzheimer's. The foundation provides scholarships and creates awareness through community outreach programs, informational sessions, and health fairs (Providence, RI). (www.alzcure.org)

Jennifer Shimkus is the Executive Director of **Rhode Islanders Sponsoring Education**, which provides scholarships and mentoring to children of incarcerated parents in order to break the intergenerational cycle of poverty, crime, and addiction. (www.riseonline.org)

Melissa Simmermaker volunteers with **Everybody Wins! Iowa**, an organization that matches elementary school students with volunteers for one-on-one sessions in which the volunteers read aloud to the students. Their goal is to instill within children a love of reading and improved reading skills, while boosting the morale of employees that participate. (www.everybodywinsiowa.org)

Kayleen Simmons is the Founder and Executive Director of **People Helping People** (Salt Lake City, UT), a group that helps low-income women and single mothers secure better-paying jobs and break the cycle of poverty. With the help of People Helping People, one woman was able to double her salary, triple her 401(k) contribution, and buy a home. (www.mentors4women.org)

Carol Singer and **Syd Singer** are the Director and President Emeritus of the Board, respectively, of **Veterans Place** (Pittsburgh, PA), a transitional housing center that was established by a group of veterans to help fellow veterans in need. Veterans Place provides a residence for homeless former veterans, along with job train-ing and psychological support as they are reintegrated into the community. (www.veteransplace.org)

Beth Smith is the Executive Director of **Winners Circle** (Omaha, NE), an organization that encourages and rewards student achievement through a program of goal-setting and celebrating accomplishments. Volunteer "Goal Buddies" visit classrooms to support and motivate students, as well as reward them with medals during Winners Circle celebrations. (www.winners-circle.org)

Clinton Smith is a volunteer with the Senior Outreach Services program at **University of Nevada Reno's Sanford Center for Aging.** This program helps frail seniors live independently by matching them with senior volunteers who provide assistance and companionship. (www.unr.edu/hcs/scag/volunteer/sos.html)

Wally Smith volunteers for the **Allen County Citizens Emergency Response Team (CERT)** . When the St. Mary's River flooded in 2003, Wally was instrumental in mobilizing over six hundred volunteers and leading them in the flood-fighting efforts at the water line. He is also a nationally certified CERT trainer (IN). (www.fwachomeland.org/index.php?option=com_content&task=view&id=41&Itemid=50)

Heather Soener is the Executive Director of **Young Women's Resource Center** (Des Moines, IA), which utilizes a gender-specific curriculum to support and educate young women ages 11-21 as they grow and experience life's challenges. Heather's center offers parenting and childbirth education for young pregnant women and promotes positive relationships and self-esteem. (www.ywrc.org)

Nevzer Stacey is the President and Founder of **HasNa**, which promotes cross-cultural understanding and economic empowerment in culturally divided areas of the world (Cyprus, Turkey, US) and encourages individuals and communities to work together toward advancement and peaceful coexistence. (www.hasna.org)

Tammy Stalzer serves patients and families affected by ALS (amyotrophic lateral sclerosis), or Lou Gehrig's disease, through **ALS in the Heartland** (Omaha, NE). This organization provides equipment such as wheelchairs and walkers at no charge, respite care, and support groups for patients, families, and friends. (www.alsintheheartland.org)

Mark Stanzilis is an **AmeriCorps** Volunteer Coordinator and Historic Educator serving the Delaware State Parks. He educates the public about the natural, historical, and cultural resources of Cape Henlopen State Park in Lewes, and his passion is creating awareness through education. (www.americorps.gov)

Ian Storrar is the Chief Operating Officer of **Mobilize.org**, an all-partisan network dedicated to educating, empowering, and energizing young people to increase their civic engagement and political participation. The organization started with a group of UC Berkeley students traveling to Sacramento to lobby on issues affecting students in California, and later expanded to the DC area. (www.mobilize.org)

Doug Sudell is CEO for **HandsOn Hartford** (CT), and he is breaking the mold on how non-profits raise money. Instead of relying on grants and donations, he facilitated the purchase of a Huntington Learning Center franchise to not only serve the community better but also help financially support their other projects. (www.handsonhartford.org)

Bailey T. Susic is the Program Outreach Coordinator at **Pro Bono Counseling Project** (Baltimore, MD) which provides uninsured or low-income individuals and families with mental health care provided by volunteer, licensed mental health professionals. This organization particularly helps those who earn too much to qualify for state mental health benefits, but cannot afford to pay for counseling on their own. (www.probonocounseling.org)

Yvette Sutton, businesswoman and mother of 7, helped start **Culture Inc.**, (Des Moines, IA) an afterschool arts program that includes music production, graphic design, art, dance, photography, filmmaking, poetry, and drama. Culture Inc. supports creative expression, teamwork, and acceptance of cultural diversity, and supple-ments school systems that are experiencing budget cuts in fine arts programs. (www.cultureincorporated.org)

Stephanie Swanson volunteers for **Desert Ministries**, an organization that arranges weekly visits to Omaha elderly in nursing homes. Desert Ministries values the life and wisdom of the elderly and seeks to bring "hope through love" to nursing home residents. (www.desertministries.org)

Donna Taglianetti is the Executive Director of **Co-opportunity** (Hartford, CT) which empowers low-income people to become self-sufficient community stakeholders through housing and economic development programs. Through Co-opportunity, Donna helps community members achieve long-term economic well-being and stability. (www.co-opportunity.org)

Linda Thibodeau is the President of the Board of Directors of **Leave Out Violence (LOVE)** (Canada & NYC) which empowers young people to discuss alternatives to violence with their peers. Linda's stepmother started LOVE after Linda's father was fatally stabbed by a 14-year-old boy in search of drug money. LOVE's photography and writing programs help teens who have been affected by violence to express themselves. (www.leaveoutviolence-us.org)

Donald Thornton led creative efforts to establish bowling events for the blind through the local chapter of **Friends of the Blind and Disabled**. His group picks up sight-impaired individuals and takes them out for a fun evening of bowling. Don also distributes food and household supplies at the local food bank and serves on the board of the local Kiwanis Club volunteer center.

Julie Trell works for **Salesforce.com**, a San Francisco company that received the 2009 Corporate Engagement Award from the Points of Light Institute for its outstanding employee volunteer program. From 2000 to 2009, 85% of Salesforce.com employees have collectively donated over 140,000 hours of their time in community service. (www.salesforce.com)

Tom Tuohy is the Founder of **Dreams for Kids**, an organization that started in 1989 when Tom and his friends visited a Chicago homeless shelter to deliver presents to the kids on Christmas Eve. As of 2009, Dreams for Kids has a presence in over thirty countries and has impacted 28,000 children through its programs. (www.dreamsforkids.org)

Karen Van Dyke is the President and Treasurer of **Educate Uganda**, which consists of a sponsorship program and a school improvement program. Through sponsorships, Karen's organization (Omaha, NE) pays the school fees of children who have lost one or both of their parents. The school improvement program identifies and implements much-needed changes, such as the construction of classrooms and latrines. (www.educateuganda.org)

Sina Ward is the volunteer manager for the Senior Outreach Services program at **University of Nevada Reno's Sanford Center for Aging.** This program helps frail seniors live independently by matching them with senior volunteers who provide assistance and companionship. (www.unr.edu/hcs/scag/volunteer/sos.html)

Dr. Hattie Washington (Baltimore, MD) is the Founder and President of **Aunt Hattie's Place**, which provides a safe, stable, nurturing and long-term home for abused, abandoned, or neglected children in foster care. In 2009, Aunt Hattie's Place housed 18 young boys who entered with psychological and behavioral problems. Thanks to Aunt Hattie, the boys have made significant progress in their academics, behavior, and self-esteem. (www.aunthattie.homestead.com)

Linda Watson-Patterson is a project leader for the **Greater Philadelphia Cares** Discovery program, a science enrichment program at a local elementary school. She also volunteers with Jazz Bridge, an organization that assists jazz musicians in times of crisis, and Opportunities, PA, which helps homeless young adults become self-sufficient. (www.philacares.com)

Melvina Weaver is Afterschool Program Operations Manager at **Education Works**, which provides educational programs and services in communities confronting high rates of poverty and other barriers to educational achievement. Melvina's work strengthens and reinforces academics, recreational and interpersonal skills of K–12 students. (www.educationworks-online.org/index2asp)

Karen Webb volunteers at **Utah Hospice Specialists**, where she provides respite care and helps patients and their families compile their stories and pictures into a hardbound "Memory Book." When a patient passes away, the volunteer's involvement usually ceases, but Karen continues to assist a former patient's widow by running errands and helping around the house. (www.hospicespecialists.com)

Tyler Weig is Executive Director of **Everybody Wins! Iowa**, an organization that matches elementary school students with volunteers for one-on-one sessions in which the volunteers read aloud to the students. Their goal is to instill within children a love of reading and improved reading skills, while boosting the morale of employees that participate. (www.everybodywinsiowa.org)

Chris Weske is a member of the Board of Directors of **Sacramento Children's Home**, an organization that has provided a host of programs and services to help abused or at-risk children, as well as families in crisis, for over one hundred and forty years. (www.kidshome.org)

Kimberly Williams is CEO of **Boys and Girls Club of Greater Sacramento**, which provides youth with a safe environment to participate in positive, fun activities that help young people set and reach their goals. (www.bgcsac.org)

Creighton Wong works with the **Challenged Athletes Foundation** (San Diego, CA) to fundraise for children who are amputees, so that they have access to prosthetics and can compete in sports. Creighton is a triathlete who also happens to be a congenital amputee. (www.challengedathletes.org)

Brian Woods is the Founder and Executive Director of the **Metropolitan Community Services T.O.U.C.H. inmate mentoring program**. Brian's organization assists prisoners with reintegration into society through mentoring, life skills training, and employment opportunities. The purpose of T.O.U.C.H. is to lower recidivism rates and develop law-abiding, responsible men and women. (Columbus, OH) (www.touchimp.org)

Linda Wuestenberg co-founded **Parent Grief** and **MyEmergencyContact Info.org** after losing her son, Steve, in a car accident. Linda and her husband were not notified until seven hours after the accident, because emergency responders did not have access to Steve's emergency contacts. Parent Grief worked with Ohio lawmakers to establish the Ohio Next of Kin Database, so that individuals can enter emergency contact information into the system. (www.myemergencycontactinfo.org)

Steveanna Wynn is the Executive Director of **SHARE Food Program**, which provides food for 550 food distribution centers per week. With 2,000 volunteers, the program reaches out to 100,000 families in 5 different states (DE, MD, NJ, NY, PA). (www.sharefoodprogram.org)

As of 2009, **Penn Yee** had volunteered with the **Sacramento Police Department** for 12 years, with the Neighborhood Resource Center and Volunteer in Patrol (VIP) program. Penn has contributed nearly three thousand volunteer hours and is dedicated to supporting the patrol activities of the local police department. (www.sacpd.org)

INDEX

"Colorado" continues next page

E

F

G

T

"Trails" continues next page

U

V

W

Y

EPILOGUE

Thank you so much for reading ***Extra Mile America:*** *Stories of Inspiration, Possibility and Purpose.* I hope that the stories in this book have touched your spirit; I hope that they have inspired you to adopt the *"go the extra mile"* message as your own.

With few exceptions, we all want more out of life. We all chase the dream of wanting something better for ourselves, for our families, for our employers, and for our communities. *"Going the extra mile"* in personal effort is the only way I know that legitimizes our ability to affect the results in each of these areas.

The change we seek in our lives...at home, at work, and in our communities...begins with us as individuals. It begins with the attitudes we carry and the actions we take. It begins with us *"going the extra mile."*

I hope you choose the best for yourself in life. I hope, too, that you recognize your power in making that happen..

"Go the extra mile"...and create a great life!

P.S. If you are a kindred spirit in the "go the extra mile" theme, and if you have experienced the "go the extra mile" principle in its full power, I would love to hear from you! Write to me and share your story.

Or...if you know of an individual or organization who has made a difference because of an extra-mile effort, share with me that story as well!

Shawn@ShawnAnderson.com

Shawn Anderson is a writer and national speaker on the topic of "possibility thinking and creating opportunity." Dedicated to assisting others to maximize potential, Shawn has a life mission of empowering 1,000,000 people to lead a more positive and purposeful existence.

At his core, Shawn has always been an entrepreneur. From his first business selling night crawlers to fishermen at age ten, Shawn has proven his resourcefulness in building successful organizations, developing national events, and creating a multi-million dollar business from the ground floor. A graduate of the University of California at Berkeley, he is a solidifier of ideas and a magnifier of projects. Shawn's books include:

Countdown to College: *Preparing Your Student for Success in the Collegiate Universe*

SOAR to the TOP: *Rise Above the Crowd and Fly Away to Your Dream*

Amicus 101: *A Story About the Pursuit of Purpose and Overcoming Life's Chaos*

Lessons From A. Friend: *A Guided Journal Through the Lessons of Amicus 101*

Extra Mile America: *Stories of Inspiration, Possibility and Purpose*

Shawn also mails out a weekly online motivational newsletter to readers called the *M.A.P. to Success Circle!* which is dedicated to assisting readers to build "Momentum in Attitude and Possibility."

For more, go to:

www.ShawnAnderson.com OR www.ExtraMileAmerica.com

Boston Mayor Thomas M. Menino: "I'm pleased Shawn will conclude his extraordinary cross-country bike ride in Boston. Not only is Boston a bike-friendly city, but it's a place where volunteerism makes an impact on our community every day."

Warwick, Rhode Island Mayor Scott Avedisian: "From those who give their time as volunteers in Warwick schools, to our seniors who spend thousands of hours each year at hospitals and nonprofit agencies, and from citizens of every age who participate in civic groups to our City Year corps activities, the City of Warwick is a community that prides itself on volunteerism. I'm proud to recognize... Extra Mile Day...and applaud Shawn Anderson for his remarkable and inspiring efforts to spotlight the selfless works of people throughout the US."

Little Rock, Arkansas Mayor Mark Stodola: "...We take Shawn Anderson's message to heart; that is why we go the extra mile to instill a passion for volunteering and an orientation toward service in our youth. The Youth Council I lead allows high school students in Little Rock to participate in volunteer projects and learn how to make the community a better place. We are happy to lend our support to Shawn Anderson and his Extra Mile America Tour."

Colorado State Representative John M. Kefalas: "Volunteerism and civic engagement are key elements of a healthy, compassionate, and vibrant community that works together for the common good. ...Fort Collins...exemplifies these qualities in the highest degree as we work to address the problems and issues that many...face. ...Shawn Anderson is another wonderful example of the human spirit carrying the message that we are all in this together while shining light on local heroes and organizations doing the good works."

Reno Mayor Bob Cashell: "We are honored that [Shawn] has selected Reno as one of the 21 cities.... We certainly have a number of outstanding citizens here who go 'the extra mile' to make our community a better place for everyone. Shawn and local heroes... including the residents of Reno, show one person can really make a difference."

Congresswoman Barbara Lee, U.S. House of Representatives: "Oakland is filled with 'extra mile people' working hard every day to make their community a better place. We are happy to welcome Shawn Anderson...and support his mission to acknowledge local heros across the country and inspire Americans to do more to help each other."

Arizona State Senator Amanda Aguirre: "It is energizing to hear stories of people going the extra mile with positive action in their lives. We see it daily in the stories of the men, women and children in Arizona. I congratulate Shawn Anderson on his quest to bike across America with the Extra Mile America Tour and wish him the best on his journey."

Hawaii State Representative Karen Awana: "As our country embarks on uncertain times, the Extra Mile America Tour...acknowledges those who keep pace and continue to sacrifice their time toward the betterment of their neighborhood, county and state. Shawn Anderson exemplifies this worthy initiative....No task is too difficult if performed by all. The State of Hawaii commends Shawn for his leadership and extends best wishes to others who strive to make their community a better place."

Houston Councilmember Pam Holm: "Recognition of volunteerism, particularly during the economic times of today, is a noble cause. Volunteers are noble; they give of their time and resources with no expectation of a return and often without notice or recognition. Shawn Anderson reminds each of us, one person makes a difference; one person helping another person quickly builds a strong team."